Its Origin and Use

Written by
DAVID BERNARD
C.A. BREWER
G. W. HASSEBROCK
DAN SEGRAVES

This book is designed for personal or group study.

PENTECOSTAL PUBLISHING HOUSE
8855 DUNN ROAD
HAZELWOOD, MO 63042-2299

Word Aflame Elective Series

The Bible: Its Origin and Use

WHY? A Study of Christian Standards
Spiritual Growth and Maturity
Bible Doctrines: Foundation of the Church
Strategy for Life for Singles and Young Adults
Your New Life
Purpose at Sunset
Values That Last
Meet the United Pentecostal Church International
Facing the Issues
Life's Choices
Alive in the Spirit
A Look at Stewardship
A Look at Pentecostal Worship
Financial Planning for Successful Living

Family Life Selections

The Christian Youth
The Christian Woman
The Christian Man
The Christian Parent

EDITORIAL STAFF

R. M. Davis . . . . Editor
P. D. Buford . . . . Associate Editor

J. L. Hall . . . . Editor in Chief
United Pentecostal Church International

©1985 by the Pentecostal Publishing House, Hazelwood, Missouri. All rights reserved.
Reprint History: 1985, 1994, 1995, 1999, 2004
ISBN 1-56722-051-7

CURRICULUM COMMITTEE: James E. Boatman, P. D. Buford, Daniel L. Butler, R. M. Davis, Gary D. Erickson, Jack C. Garrison, J. L. Hall, G. W. Hassebrock, Garth E. Hatheway, Vernon D. McGarvey, David L. Reynolds, Charles A. Rutter, R. L. Wyser.

Foreword

**Richard M. Davis
Editor
Word Aflame Publications**

"Who am I? How did I get here? What is my purpose in life?"

Mankind has pondered these and other questions from the earliest times of civilization. Innate within an individual is a desire for understanding the purpose of existence. Of paramount importance to every human being is the ability to discover and fulfill his place in society.

Answering and dealing with each of these and other questions of life, the Bible stands tall and in a class all its own. Men who were inspired of God produced the Bible, the one single greatest piece of literature ever provided to mankind. The Bible continues to remain the top selling book of the ages.

Standing as a testimony to the sacred sanction of the Bible as God's Word is the miraculous way in which the many scriptural writings have been brought together into one unified book of truth. It can be nothing short of miraculous that so many writers from so many diverse backgrounds and with such extreme personalities were each used of God to write the supreme book of all time.

Second only to the way in which God caused His Word to be recorded and brought together into one book is the miraculous way in which He has caused

His Word to be preserved for all generations. Though hated and attacked by critics and unbelievers of every age, the Bible has survived each attack. Copied and translated from generation to generation and from language to language, the Bible lives on today while those who have fought it lie in their tombs, reserved for the last judgment.

Yet another testimony to the unimpeachable character and truth of the Holy Bible is its continued life-changing impact upon the lives of those who read and obey it. It is the greatest manual for living, the most practical self-improvement book, and the most inspiring positive mental attitude book ever written. All the answers of life for which men search may be discovered within its sacred pages. In the Bible lie the treasures of the abundant life Jesus Christ came to give.

In this study you will marvel at the pervasive scope of the plan of God as displayed through His Word. You will be both amazed and inspired as you discover how God's Word was written and how He brought it all together. You will learn how to study, memorize, and rightly divide God's Word.

Perhaps most importantly, we can better learn how to apply God's Word to our lives. It is indeed God's blueprint for living and can give every Christian the spiritual direction he needs in life.

May the Holy Spirit direct you as you study about God's Word to mankind—the Bible. May this book help to generate a revival of reverence and awe for the greatest Book ever given to humanity.

Contents

Chapter	Page

Foreword 3
1. The Voice of Authority 7
2. The Bible—The Word of God 19
3. Surveying the Word 30
4. The Complete Word 43
5. Preserving the Word 56
6. Translating the Word 69
7. Hiding the Word....................82
8. Studying the Word..................92
9. Rightly Dividing the Word 103
10. Believing the Word 115
11. Proving the Word..................126
12. Applying the Word.................137
13. Doctrine—God's Blueprint for Living 149

The Voice of Authority

1

> *"For we dare not make ourselves of the number, or compare ourselves with some that commend themselves: but they measuring themselves by themselves, and comparing themselves among themselves, are not wise."*
>
> *II Corinthians 10:12*

Start with the Scriptures

Deuteronomy 4:2
Psalm 119:89
Matthew 7:28-29

I Corinthians 1; 2
Galatians 4:6-9
Revelation 22:18-19

What a day in which we live! It is a day of immodesty and immorality, a day of violence and vulgarity, a day of permissiveness and pornography. Traditional values regarding such subjects as marriage and responsibility to children are challenged by the lifestyles of many people who seem content to "do their own thing." Fathers, too often, live up to a reputation of being cruel brutes at home and licentious playboys while away from home. Women, to an alarming extent, have resisted the submissive, supportive role as designed by God, and children have followed the trend towards living only for selfish pleasure.

In a day when our society is becoming so "unglued" and "unhinged," are there any absolutes, any fundamental and ultimate truths which can hold things together? Are there any guidelines? Are there any principles that we can live and die by? Must we follow the vague and confusing philosophies of men into complete darkness and utter despair? (A number of the existentialists, for example, taught that life was futile and absurd, since there are no external standards or ethical rules, stressing that the individual is "free" to make his own choices. These existentialists not only denied God, but accepted an existence without meaning or direction.)

Situation ethics (the idea that any and every action may be justified under certain conditions) is more appealing to the natural mind than accepting responsibility for one's own actions.

There are those who teach relativism, the view that truths depend upon the person or persons holding them. Truth, for these individuals, would never be absolute.

All such natural reasoning is a human attempt to explain the meaning of life apart from God. Most people seem intent on living a life of pleasure and sin, and if they do believe in God, they prefer to think that He will somehow wink at their transgressions. After all, they reason, neighbors do some things they themselves would never think of doing. As in the chaotic days of the judges, we are approaching a moral anarchy, where every man does "that which is right in his own eyes." (See Judges 21:25.)

Truth Is Absolute

Far from catering to the changing opinions of the

day, truth stands independent of men's theories and speculations. It transcends the highest opinions of men, for truth is that which sets men free from illusion. It gives the proper perspective.

Without God, men at their best are groping in the darkness. Sin has blinded all mankind to reality, but truth has a dynamic power to set us free (John 8:32).

Why be so concerned, someone may ask, about the absolute truth? Why not be content with a degree of truth? Such an argument suggests that we should be satisfied to live in the shadows, hiding our eyes from the brilliance of God's full revelation.

Too often, men have done just that. They have mixed truth with error. They have drawn back from God when they have seen His holiness. To see God as He is demands that our lives, our strength, our all be submitted to Him. The only way to remain aligned with truth is to follow every precept of God, but the cost is great. The world, for the most part, prefers to follow the easier path of compromise and sin. "And this is the condemnation, that light is come into the world, and men loved darkness rather than light, because their deeds were evil" (John 3:19).

No, the world for the most part, has not found the way of truth. Though billions of dollars are being spent on education and research, and though amazing strides are being made in the sciences, mankind remains peculiarly confused and disorientated about the purpose and direction of life.

God alone is the source of all knowledge. "For the LORD is a God of knowledge, and by him actions are weighed" (I Samuel 2:3). The Bible offers ample evidence that "it is not in man that walketh to direct his steps" (Jeremiah 10:23), but that "the steps of a good man are ordered by the LORD" (Psalm 37:23).

Daniel and his three Hebrew friends, although captives in Babylon, were given knowledge from God Himself (Daniel 1:17). "And in all matters of wisdom and understanding, that the king enquired of them, he found them ten times better than all the magicians and astrologers that were in all his realm" (Daniel 1:20). The interpretation of Nebuchadnezzar's dream in chapter two was only possible because Daniel knew the God of wisdom and might. Through no natural wisdom of his own, Daniel interpreted a second dream of Nebuchadnezzar in chapter four; in chapter five this Hebrew astounded Belshazzar by reading the handwriting on the wall. If God could impart knowledge of such magnitude that empires were affected, surely He knows how to direct us toward reality.

Truth, the revelation of God and all things as He sees them, can only be found in the Scriptures. According to both the Old and New Testaments, God's Word brings us face to face with reality. (See Psalm 119:142; John 17:17.) The Bible does not merely contain the truth; it is the truth. God, in His infinite wisdom, chose to reveal Himself through the pages of this Book. We have no other revelation than that which God has chosen to give us. We dare not add to that revelation, nor do we dare take away from its precepts. (See Revelation 22:18-19.) The Bible is no ordinary book; it is God's Book. The Christian faith is based on its principles, and the apostles taught that God Himself is its author (I Thessalonians 2:13).

The act of God communicating His Word to humanity in direct revelation is called inspiration. It is so vital an issue that Paul the apostle defended his ministry by stating that he had not received authority from men to preach the gospel. "But I certify you, brethren, that the gospel which was preached of me is not after man. For I neither received it of man, neither was I taught it, but by the revelation of Jesus Christ" (Galatians 1:11-12).

The Holy Ghost guided the writers of the Bible into

writing exact statements of truth. Far from being the product of the human mind, the Scriptures are God-breathed, inspired by God Himself. "For the prophecy came not in old time by the will of man: but holy men of God spake as they were moved by the Holy Ghost" (II Peter 1:21).

The Confusion of the Natural Mind

In stark contrast to the authoritative voice of the Scriptures, there are various ideologies of human thinking. The Bible clearly states, "But the natural man receiveth not the things of the Spirit of God" (I Corinthians 2:14), and so it comes as no great surprise that people have conceived all manner of theories about life. There are the spiritualists who strive to communicate with the dead and the animists who attribute conscious life to rocks, streams and trees. The atheists deny the existence of God, and the agnostics teach that God, the ultimate truth, is unknowable. The humanists, despite unmistakeable evidence to the contrary, teach that mankind is essentially good and can be dignified through his own powers of reasoning.

What a conglomeration of concepts and ideals mankind has followed! The person who is always reaching for truth with his own intellect, is generally unwilling to accept the clear instruction of the infallible Word of God. That person is like a hunter lost in the woods, without compass or adequate provisions, who refuses to chart his course by the brilliant sun.

Religious Darkness

Adding to the confusion of this age is the fact that many people who profess to be leading others toward truth are themselves stumbling in the darkness. If

Jesus called the Pharisees "blind leaders of the blind" (Matthew 15:14), how would He refer to modern religionists who deny His virgin birth, His divinity and His miracles? Like the Sadducees of old, many modern clergymen "do err, not knowing the scriptures, nor the power of God" (Matthew 22:29). Emphasis is too often placed on formality and tradition, with vast sums of money being spent on church structure and decor. Instead of preaching the Word of God, such clergymen give their opinions on social issues and express their sympathy for radical left-wing or right-wing causes.

There has been a shameful departure from the Bible in many religious circles. Many religious people who would be deeply offended if they were called "non-Christian" have nevertheless strayed from the teachings of the apostles. Someone has called the cults "the unpaid debt of the church," indicating that thousands have never been reached with the truth. Indeed, many have turned to pseudo-Christianity, to yoga or to meditation out of sheer desperation. There needs to be some guidelines for living laid down from God's holy Book, the Bible; men still need to hear the very certain sound of the gospel.

Two Vital Questions

Two vital questions come to the forefront when examining religious truth. These questions, by their nature interrelated, bring us to the heart of the matter of divine inspiration. Both issues are central. They stand eternal, timeless and unchangeable.

First, the question of who Christ really is. If a person fails to comprehend this point, he fails in all, for Jesus said, "If ye believe not that I am he, ye shall die in your sins" (John 8:24).

Christian faith is irrevocably tied to the truth of Jesus Christ's nature. His majestic personality stands at the center of all divine revelation. All other lights pale in His presence, for He is the light of the world. All other truths are mere reflections of the reality called Christ. He Himself declared, "I am the truth." He did not merely give some directions as to how to find God and life. He declared Himself to be the way, the truth, and the life. In response to Philip's request, "Shew us the Father" (John 14:8), Jesus affirmed, "Have I been so long time with you, and yet hast thou not known me, Philip? he that hath seen me hath seen the Father" (John 14:9).

Jesus Christ, through His divine birth, was the very essence of God. Although a man in every sense of the word, our Lord was the perfect revelation of God. "For in him dwelleth all the fulness of the Godhead bodily" (Colossians 2:9). There can be little knowledge of God apart from the Son. "No man has seen God at any time; the only, unique Son, the only begotten God, Who is in the bosom of the Father, He has declared Him—He has revealed Him, brought Him out where He can be seen; He has interpreted Him, and He has made Him known" (John 1:18, *The Amplified Bible*). (See also Hebrews 1:1-2.)

No wonder Jesus could speak with such authority, for He was the very expression of God. He was the Word made flesh (John 1:14). When men saw Jesus, they saw the glory of God; when they heard Him speak, they marvelled at His wisdom. Even His enemies declared, "Never man spake like this man" (John 7:46).

What confidence should be shown in the words of Christ! When Jesus spoke, the wind and the sea obeyed, and with great authority He cast out devils. "And it came to pass, when Jesus had ended these sayings, the people were astonished at his doctrine: For he taught them as one having authority, and not as the scribes" (Matthew 7:28-29).

We would do well to follow the example of the centurion who sent messengers to Jesus for the healing of the servant. As Jesus approached the centurion's home, that Roman officer sent friends with a further message, "I am not worthy that thou shouldest enter under my roof. . .but say in a word, and my servant shall be healed. For I also am a man set under authority" (Luke 7:6-8).

Second, the question of whether the Bible can be trusted as the true source of divine revelation. Can we believe what the Bible teaches? Is the Bible God's Word to the exclusion of all other so-called sacred books?

Since we are dealing with eternal matters, it is absolutely necessary to know whether the Bible is exactly what it claims to be in such Scriptures as II Timothy 3:16 and II Peter 1:21. Or, if not, should some other source of revelation be depended upon, apart from the Scriptures?

The question becomes all the more important when we realize that cult members and modern theologians alike deny the integrity of the Bible. Mormons, for instance, though they use biblical terms, distrust the Bible as having been corrupted by the Roman Catholic Church. "We believe," their eighth Article of Faith states, "the Bible to be the word of God as far as it is translated correctly." Such statements tend to discredit the Bible in favor of some other source of authority. In the case of the Mormons, the other authority is the Book of Mormon, other recognized writings of Joseph Smith, and their own subjective feelings.

With arrogant assurance, others (using man-made substitutes for the Bible) will claim that they themselves are the only ones who can properly interpret the Scriptures. Charles Taze Russell, founder of the Jehovah's Witnesses, declared that it would be more worthwhile to read his seven-volume *Studies in the Scriptures* than to read the Scriptures themselves.

Modernists often argue that only certain parts of the Bible are trustworthy, but this idea certainly leads to confusion. If their idea were correct, who then would or could determine what parts contain truth and what parts contain error? How can we imagine sinners responding to a gospel which is only partially true? How can Christians have a firm foundation if their scriptural base is full of human errors? The shifting sands of modern criticism is a poor foundation upon which to build a Christian life.

For the Bible to be authoritative it must be true. There is no middle ground. A Bible that is erroneous is not sacred. If God communicated His Word to mankind, He certainly was able to avoid each and every error. The individual facts as well as the ideas expressed in the Bible are true. Unlike the absurdities expressed in other so-called sacred writings (Hindus are taught that Brahma was born in a golden egg and Zorbastrians embrace nature worship), the Bible speaks with common sense and time-tested accuracy.

There is a vibrancy and a power in the Bible as found in no other literature, whether the Koran, the writings of Confucius, or the Veda. No papal decree or visionary statement of a modern-day guru can match the sacred statements of the Bible. It speaks with divine eloquence and yet speaks with such simplicity that a little child can understand its meaning.

Jesus Christ endorsed the Scriptures. There is not a shred of evidence to suggest that Jesus doubted any of the Old Testament writings. On the contrary, the attitude shown by Jesus toward the Scriptures was absolute trust. Although He spoke sharply against the religious errors of His day, our Lord taught that the Scriptures are inerrant.

"Think not that I am come to destroy the law, or

the prophets: I am not come to destroy, but to fulfil. For verily I say unto you, Till heaven and earth pass, one jot or one tittle shall in no wise pass from the law, till all be fulfilled. Whosoever therefore shall break one of these least commandments, and shall teach men so, he shall be called the least in the kingdom of heaven: but whosoever shall do and teach them, the same shall be called great in the kingdom of heaven" (Matthew 5:17-19).

More will be said in this book regarding evidences that the Bible is true, but for the Christian the greatest proof of scriptural authority is Jesus Christ Himself. If Jesus rebuked the devil with verses from the Old Testament (Matthew 4), foretold His suffering in the light of Scriptures (Luke 18:31-34) and declared, "The scriptures must be fulfilled" (Mark 14:49), there needs to be no doubt in the mind of the believer regarding biblical authority. The unbeliever, on the other hand, often refuses to accept the authority of the Bible even when faced with infallible proofs.

Beyond all human testimony, there is the witness of the Spirit. When Jesus was on the earth He spoke of the testimony of John the Baptist as confirming the truth regarding Himself. Talking to the Jewish rulers, He declared that while John had witnessed the truth, He Himself did not accept a mere human witness. The works appointed by the Father had been accomplished in His ministry, and so the Lord Jesus declared, "The same works that I do, bear witness of me, that the Father hath sent me. And the Father himself, which hath sent me, hath borne witness of me" (John 5:36-37).

The confirmation of the Spirit of God should be adequate proof of the Bible's authority. It is difficult to argue with the saving power of the gospel when lives are dramatically changed. It was impossible for the Jewish rulers to deny the miracle-working power in the Early Church (Acts 4:16); it should prove equally futile for the world to refute the testimony of spiritual signs in these last days.

The story is told of an atheistic lecturer who spoke against the Bible and the miracles of Christ. He ridiculed the story of Christ's first miracle, that of turning water into wine. In the audience sat a former drunkard who had been touched by the delivering power of the gospel. "I don't know," he spoke out, "about turning water into wine, but I know that the Lord can turn wine into baby shoes and groceries for my table."

A preacher was once asked how he knew the Bible was true. The simple answer, "It works," was adequate. There is just nothing like experience to dispel the arguments of unbelievers. No doubt there were those who scoffed at Robert Fulton's steamship and at the Wright brothers' airship, but their ideas were proven correct in experimental tests. When God's Word is put to the actual test, it is no less trustworthy, no less authoritative, and no less truthful. "O taste and see that the LORD is good: blessed is the man that trusteth in him" (Psalm 34:8).

Test Your Knowledge

1. The _____ have often taught that there are no external standards.

2. The idea that any and every situation may be justified under certain conditions is _____ _____.

3. The view that truths depend upon the person holding them is called _____.

4. _____ is the revelation of God and all things as He sees them.

5. The _____ denies the existence of God.

6. There can be little knowledge of God apart

from the _____.

7. _____ distrust the Bible as having been corrupted by the Roman Catholic Church.

8. Charles Taze Russell declared his writings to be superior to the _____.

9. A Bible that is erroneous is not _____.

10. _____ endorsed the Scriptures.

Apply Your Knowledge

To grow spiritually, Christians not only need to accept the full authority of the Bible, but also to allow the Scriptures to change their lives. There are some steps which will help to have our minds transformed (Romans 12:2).

First, go to God in prayer and earnestly ask Him to reveal His will to you from His Word. Ask Him to penetrate deeply into your heart, exposing any sinful areas of thought, word or deed.

Then turn to your Bible and search out the very areas where you have sensed a definite weakness (e.g. temper). Your research should give you explicit guidelines for improvement and a sense of God's loving care.

Finally, thank God for a new work that He has begun in your heart.

Expand Your Knowledge

In preparation for the next chapter, read the Scriptures listed under the chapter title. Then use a good Bible concordance or W. E. Vine's *Expository Dictionary of New Testament Words* to find the meaning of the following: *revelation, inspired, moved* (as in II Peter 1:21), *word* (as in I Thessalonians 1:8 and II Thessalonians 3:1), and *mystery*.

The Bible—
The Word of God

"All scripture is given by inspiration of God, and is profitable for doctrine, for reproof, for correction, for instruction in righteousness."

II Timothy 3:16

Start with the Scriptures

Exodus 19; 31; 32   Deuteronomy 9

The procurator and his wife listened intently to the man before them. The speaker was a prisoner of Rome, but he spoke boldly and persuasively about the Christian religion. It almost seemed that they were the prisoners, and not he, held captive as they were by his powerful words.

The procurator may have once viewed this Jew as something of a curiosity, but now there was no denying the strength of his message. It cut deeply into his conscience, and the ruler trembled as the preaching Jew "reasoned of righteousness, temperance, and judgment to come" (Acts 24:25).

There is no question that Felix was deeply affected by Paul's scriptural discourse at Caesarea. There is no doubt that Paul was convincing because he himself was convinced. Although his own life stood in jeopardy, Paul the apostle was able to bring his cruel judge to a place of fear and conviction.

Such were the results wherever Paul preached the gospel. Men might reject his message, or they might accept it, but they could not remain unchanged under his gripping statements (Acts 14:1-2). Paul would preach "the word of God in the synagogues of the Jews" (Acts 13:5), powerfully demonstrating from the Old Testament that Jesus was indeed the Messiah. "And Paul, as his manner was, went in unto them, and three sabbath days reasoned with them out of the scriptures, Opening and alleging, that Christ must needs have suffered, and risen again from the dead; and that this Jesus whom I preach unto you, is Christ" (Acts 17:2-3).

Even the critics of the Bible will be forced to admit that one reason Paul the apostle had such a profound effect upon the world was because he thoroughly trusted the Scriptures. In a very clear statement to young Timothy, whom he was strengthening in the work of the Lord, Paul declared, "All scripture is given by inspiration of God" (II Timothy 3:16).

The Revelation of God

How else could man hope to know the God "that dwellest in the heavens" (Psalm 123:1) except by revelation? If as the Bible asserts, God's ways are not our ways and His thoughts not our thoughts (Isaiah 55:8-9), then surely man could never understand the divine plan simply by means of human ability. As Paul told the Corinthians, God has chosen to disclose Himself through His Spirit. "But as it is written, Eye hath not seen, nor ear heard, neither have entered into the heart of man, the things which God hath prepared for them that love him: But God hath revealed them unto us by his Spirit: for the Spirit searcheth all things, yea, the deep things of God" (I Corinthians 2:9-10).

What human reason alone has failed to provide, God in His mercy, has supplied through revelation.

This special revelation goes beyond the fact that God exists—nature tells us that—and speaks to us of the redemptive plan. Its central theme is Christ, the one who saves sinful mankind from an eternal death. This revelation is an unveiling or self-disclosing of the thoughts and intents of God to men.

Inspiration Defined

As in the case of all major biblical doctrines, the matter of inspiration has been challenged by skeptics and unbelievers. Since the Bible is a spiritual book of many pages, it should not seem strange that critics have challenged many parts of the Scriptures which they either are unwilling or unable to understand.

Inspiration may be defined as the direct influence of God on holy men in the writing of the Scriptures. The Greek word *theopneustos,* used in II Timothy 3:16, is a combination of two words: *Theos,* meaning "God," and *pneustos,* meaning "breathed." The biblical view of inspiration, then, does not entail human genius or natural inspiration. The idea of inspiration in the Scriptures means "God-breathed," thus leaving no question of the origin of the Bible.

The very words of God are written in the Bible. While some would argue that the words themselves are not inspired, only the thoughts behind them, the

Scriptures themselves are clear on this point. There are over 2,000 references in the Old Testament where the writers claimed the words were from God. The Apostle Paul, in the New Testament, was just as emphatic: "If any man think himself to be a prophet, or spiritual, let him acknowledge that the things that I write unto you are the commandments of the Lord" (I Corinthians 14:37).

Inspiration is clearly more than just a limited influence from God. It is the transmission of God's thoughts to mankind and a direct revelation of His will.

It is important to note that while God inspired the writers of the Scriptures, these men were not simply robots. They wrote in their own peculiar styles in the current language of their day. The Holy Ghost did move on them, to be sure, and kept their words unadulterated from error. And so they spoke truth—untarnished truth—which is "profitable for doctrine, for reproof, for correction, for instruction in righteousness" (II Timothy 3:16).

The Bible declares itself to be the Word of God. That fact is certain. Consistently claiming to speak the very words of God, the Old Testament prophets over and over again declared, "Thus saith the LORD." Some of David's last words were "The Spirit of the LORD spake by me, and his word was in my tongue" (II Samuel 23:2). Jeremiah was instructed, "Whatsoever I command thee thou shalt speak" (Jeremiah 1:7), and "I have put my words in thy mouth" (Jeremiah 1:9).

The New Testament writers also identified Scripture with divine revelation. In I Thessalonians 2:13 believers were commended by The Apostle Paul: "When ye received the word of God which ye heard of us, ye received it not as the word of men, but as it is in truth, the word of God." Jesus Christ declared, "The scripture cannot be broken" (John

10:35), and "All things must be fulfilled, which were written in the law of Moses, and in the prophets, and in the psalms, concerning me" (Luke 24:44).

Christ, the Central Theme

Not only did Jesus Christ speak of the Scriptures in the highest of terms, but the Scriptures, in their turn, exalt Jesus Christ. In fact, Christ is the central theme of the entire Bible. He is seen as the great unifying center of the creation (Colossians 1:15-17), the grand subject of the prophets (Isaiah 53), and the head of the church (Colossians 1:18).

How can anyone read the Bible honestly and still doubt the supremacy of Jesus Christ? If we speak of royalty, He is the "King of kings"; if we speak of authority, He is the "Lord of lords." We are assured that God will not give His glory to another, and yet we read of men falling down in worship to Jesus Christ (Matthew 14:33; Luke 24:52; John 20:28). There can be no other conclusion from a reading of the Word of God but that Jesus was God "manifest in the flesh" (I Timothy 3:16).

An attack on the Word of God is an attack on the person of Jesus Christ. Brazenly, the critics have taught the fallibility of the Bible. Passing judgment on the Scriptures, they may or may not have realized what they were doing. Their criticisms have the effect, however, of subtracting from the deity of Jesus Christ. While they may say some fine things about the Lord, they would strip Him of His essential power.

Denying the reliability of the Bible they go on to reject the miracles of both the Old and New Testaments. The virgin birth and the resurrection of Jesus Christ become targets of their malicious reasoning. Paul, prophesying of these last days, warned us of those, "Having a form of godliness, but denying the power thereof: from such turn away" (II Timothy 3:5).

The Inerrant Word of God

Inerrancy is the belief that the Scriptures are trustworthy, free from error as a whole and in all their parts. Biblical statements are considered absolutely true, regardless of the subject with which they deal. Not only does the Bible teach truth regarding religion, but it is infallible on all matters, including history, science and prophecy.

There are those who claim to believe in a limited inerrancy, but this type of doctrine is dangerous to the extreme. As Harold Lindsell points out in *God's Incomparable Word* (Victor Books, S. P. Publications Inc., Box 1825, Wheaton, Illinois 60187), such thinking leads to spiritual ruin for several reasons. One reason is that God, the author of the Bible, is assumed to have made false or erroneous statements; another is that the human element is too highly regarded—people are thought of as having authored the Scriptures, rather than the Spirit of God, as was the case (II Peter 1:21).

Skepticism is nothing new. Critics of the Bible have tried over the years to produce items from the Bible which they consider proof of errancy. Strangely, much of the criticism comes from the higher halls of religious learning. A doctorate does not insure a purity of faith anymore than an insurance policy guarantees a long life. The door to spiritual truth opens only to those who have faith in the Word of God; it closes firmly on those who insist on judging the Bible by their own preconceived standards.

Quite frankly, after nearly two thousand years, the critics have failed to produce seriously damaging evidence against the reliability of the Bible. Often what may have appeared to have been errors prove in time to be authenticated by further research or by archeology. For instance, as Sidney Collett explains in *All About the Bible* (Fleming H. Revell Company, Westwood, New Jersey), the name of Belshazzar, the King of the Chaldeans, was nowhere to be found in any history apart from the record in the book of Daniel. What appeared to be a complete list of Babylonian kings excluded Belshazzar's name and, in fact, named Nabonidus as the reigning monarch. The case may have been closed as far as the critics were concerned, but in 1854 Sir Henry Rawlinson discovered some terra-cotta cylinders which mentioned in an inscription, "Belshazzar, my eldest son."

A further discovery of cuneiform tablets in 1876 revealed that, though Nabonidus had fled Babylon and had been taken prisoner by the Persians, on a particular "night. . .the king died." Since Nabonidus is known to have lived for a number of years after his empire fell, the king who died was no doubt Belshazzar, acting as regent for his father. Belshazzar's offer to make Daniel "the third ruler in the kingdom" (Daniel 5:16) is a remarkable confirmation of the biblical account. Nabonidus would have been first, Belshazzar second, and Daniel third.

The Manuscripts

Critics are prone to point out the fact that the original autographs have perished. The moist climate of Palestine in time worked havoc on the original manuscripts of the Old Testament. Moreover, the Jewish scribes, regarding the Scriptures with an almost superstitious awe, buried any manuscripts which were showing great age—lest the material upon which the Lord's holy name was written should be misused.

What remains are copies of the Old Testament

originals, but it should be noted that the early Jewish scribes followed a very rigid set of regulations when making copies of the Scriptures. One group of scribes, the Massoretes, are known to have numbered each verse, word and letter which they copied. So concerned were they with textual purity that the Massoretes counted the number of times each letter was used in a book and calculated the middle letter in that book.

Christians not only affirm that God inspired the original writers but also believe men were motivated to faithfully preserve them. The Bible was translated into various languages by early Christians, and textual criticism has served to confirm the reliability of the manuscripts (rather than discredit them). What few textual differences have been discovered do not affect the essential doctrines or commandments of the Lord.

The Written Word

The writing of the Scriptures is a remarkable tale of sacrifice and devotion. Although it is not known who all the original writers were, there is a unity of thought and of purpose throughout. The great Author of heaven directed some thirty-six to forty writers of various backgrounds to compile the greatest book ever written.

The Word of God came to patriarchs (Genesis 15:1), to prophets (Numbers 22:38, Hebrews 1:1), and to kings (II Chronicles 7:12-22). It was faithfully recorded by such notable figures as Moses, educated in an Egyptian court, and by lesser known personalities such as Amos, a herdsman of sheep and goats.

Much of what Moses wrote he received amidst the smoke and thundering of Mount Sinai, where the law of God was given. The twelve historical books, from

Joshua to Esther, were often written as eyewitness accounts of events covering some 1,000 years. The books of poetry, Job through Song of Solomon, are reflective in nature and express the deepest of human emotions. The prophets, those bold spokesmen for God, forcefully warned the disobedient of impending judgment and predicted a national restoration through the Messiah.

Firsthand accounts and personal experiences were the order of the day in the New Testament. The greatest biography ever written can be found in the gospels of four men who personally knew Jesus Christ. The clearest picture of the first century church is given by Luke in the Book of Acts. At least four of Paul's epistles (Colossians, Philemon, Ephesians, and Philippians) were written while that great apostle was a prisoner. Several of the general epistles (notably II Peter and Jude) seem to indicate that the writers themselves were struggling at the time with false teachers. Revelation, the final book of the Bible, was written by John as an exile on the island of Patmos and describes his vision of Christ.

An Incomparable Book

The Bible, because of its outstanding composition, has been called the "Miracle of the Ages." Consider the fact that it was recorded with at least ten media, from papyrus to rocks, pen to chisel, leather to clay. Then, too, it was written over a period of sixteen centuries from the first writer to the last (Moses writing about 1500 B.C. to John about A.D. 100—the span would be even longer if Job was written in patriarchal times, about 2,000 B.C.).

The scope of the biblical account is simply gigantic. Every conceivable subject is covered, using a vast range of literary style (poetry, prose, romance, mystery, biography, science, history, etc.). More than that, the Bible has a cast of characters numbered at 2,930, and some 1,551 geographical sites are listed as scenes of action. Using three languages (Hebrew, Aramaic and Greek), the writers take us from the very beginning of human history into our glorious future.

With incomparable candor the Bible tells the tale of tragedy and triumph, of cowardly betrayal and heroic exploits, of terrible defeat and tremendous victory. The sins and failures of even the heroes are recorded with crystal-clear clarity. There are no exaggerations in the sacred account; the facts speak more powerfully to the human conscience than any work of fiction possibly could. Character descriptions in the Bible are terse and to the point.

The Bible is first of all a book about God. It is an unfolding and progressive revelation of God to humanity. Whereas some people falsely say that the Bible is the record of man searching for the divine, the sacred text declares just the opposite: God, over the ages, has been faithful to declare Himself to mankind. "God, who at sundry times and in divers manners spake in time past unto the fathers by the prophets, Hath in these last days spoken unto us by his Son" (Hebrews 1:1-2).

What could be grander than God's own expression of love? Who better could speak to the broken hearts of men than the One who made men? The unveiling of God to men lifts humanity above all the creation of this world (Psalm 8:3-5). Through God's Word we are encouraged to share in the full benefits of salvation and spiritual sonship. How we should treasure the Bible, believe it and obey it!

Test Your Knowledge

What is the Word of God called in the following verses?

1. Psalm 119:105 _____
2. Ephesians 6:17_____
3. Luke 8:11 _____
4. I Peter 2:2 _____
5. Hebrews 4:12b _____

What does the Word of God do according to the following verses?

6. Psalm 119:9 _____
7. Psalm 107:20 _____
8. Psalm 19:11 _____
9. I Peter 1:23 _____
10. Psalm 19:8 _____

Apply Your Knowledge

Perhaps the best application that can be made of the Word of God is simply to read it daily and obey its precepts. Apart from messages which you may hear from ministers in a pulpit, do your own personal studies. Study the Bible by topic (e.g. sanctification, joy, warfare); study the great characters of the Bible (e.g. David, Paul the apostle); study the individual books of the Bible.

Study the Scriptures with reference material such as a Bible dictionary and a Bible concordance, but above all, study with a teachable attitude. Allow the Holy Ghost to lead you and guide you into all truth (John 16:13). When God does speak to you through His Word, underline the key Scriptures and make personal notes for your own future reference.

Expand Your Knowledge

Read "Start With the Scriptures" for the next chapter. Note that the Bible does have natural divisions of its own. Perhaps you could make a summary of each of the main divisions, listing the books within each division and the characteristics of these books.

3 Surveying the Word

> "Search the scriptures; for in them ye think ye have eternal life: and they are they which testify of me."
>
> *John 5:39*

Start with the Scriptures

Jeremiah 31:31-33
Matthew 5:17
Luke 16:16; 24:27, 44-45
John 21:25

Galatians 3:24
II Timothy 2:15
Hebrews 8:6-13; 9:15-20
II Peter 3:15-16

The Bible is like a gigantic jigsaw puzzle with 31,173 pieces. (There are that many verses in 1,189 chapters of 66 books.) Puzzles may be enjoyable, but imagine the frustrating challenge it would be to fit the pieces together if a person did not know what the overall picture was supposed to look like. It makes all the difference when the entire picture can be seen.

This chapter might be considered the picture on the front of the puzzle box. It will be a panoramic survey of the overall "picture," showing how to fit the pieces of the Bible puzzle together.

Fitting the Bible together into a picture is complicated by its size. Its cast of almost 3,000 people named and its list of over 1,550 geographical sites mentioned further complicate the picture. Other complicating factors include the Bible's ancient Eastern customs and manners, its time span of 1,600 years, and its many subjects.

People sometimes pick up pieces of the jigsaw puzzle here and there, listening to a sermon at church, reading a passage of Scripture now and then, skipping around for their devotions, collecting piece after piece. They sometimes remember isolated events and characters but often become confused trying to keep it all in order. New initiates just becoming interested in the Bible can be so overwhelmed by the enormity of the mystery that they are tempted to abandon the task.

False teachers can also lead many astray by selecting certain pieces of the puzzle—Scripture verses out of their context that do not really fit together. All false doctrines, cults and false denominations exist because of ignorance of the Scriptures. Not knowing the overall picture of the puzzle, false prophets ignore some passages and present bits and pieces of selected verses without regard to their true place in the total plan.

A major key to "rightly dividing the word of truth" (II Timothy 2:15) is simply knowing how the Bible is divided.

The Two Testaments

The sixty-six books of the Bible are divided with thirty-nine books comprising the Old Testament and twenty-seven the New Testament. These testaments represent two covenants God made with His people.

The first covenant, called *the* covenant since Moses' day (Exodus 24:8), centers around the Law given at Mount Sinai. Later Jeremiah prophesied that the Lord would replace it with a "new covenant" (Jeremiah 31:31), which Jesus announced at His last supper (Matthew 26:28). We now refer to the Sinai covenant as the Old Testament and the latter one as the New Testament. (Also see I Corinthians 11:23-25; II Corinthians 3:3, 6; Hebrews 8:6; 9:15.)

There is no contradiction between the two Testaments. Nor does the new replace or do away with the old, but rather the new *fulfills* the old (Matthew 5:17). In the famous words of Augustine, "the Old Testament [is] revealed in the New, the New veiled in the Old. . . ." Another writer says, "The New is contained in the Old and the Old is explained in the New."

The basic principles of God and moral standards do not change; truth remains the same whether it is taught from the Old Testament or the New Testament. And it is the same God in both; Jehovah of the Old Testament is Jesus Christ in the New Testament.

The basic difference between the Old Testament and the New is that the laws of God were written in stone for the Old, and now they are written on the fleshly tables of our hearts for the New. (See Jeremiah 31:33; Ezekiel 11:19-20; Ezekiel 36:26-27; II Corinthians 3:3.) The symbolic worship of the tabernacle sacrificial system, anticipating by faith the coming promise, is fulfilled in the New Testament.

Arrangement of the Old Testament Books

The Jews first divided the Old Testament books into the Law and the Prophets, then later grouped them into three classifications: the Law, the Prophets, and the Writings—arranging the order of the books by the rank of the writer. This division into "the Law and the prophets" is referred to several times by Jesus (Luke 16:16; John 1:45; Matthew 7:12; Matthew 11:13), and the three-fold division is mentioned by Jesus in Luke 24:44: "All things must be fulfilled, which were written in the law of Moses, and in the prophets, and in the psalms, concerning me."

When the Hebrews translated the Old Testament books into Greek around 200 B.C., producing the Septuagint, the order of the books was regrouped and reclassified into a new arrangement, topically, by subject matter. This Septuagint was the translation most commonly used in the time of Christ and the founding of the New Testament Church; therefore its topical pattern was widely accepted by the early Christians and has remained the traditional and popular pattern still in use today.

It is not strange to hear claims that the Jews had only twenty-two or twenty-four books in the Old Testament. The Hebrews combined some of the books that are now separated into different books. Lamentations, for instance, is added to the end of Jeremiah and Ruth is a part of the scroll of the Judges in the Hebrew Scriptures. Actually they have the same Scriptures, the same identical thirty-nine books with every verse that we have now.

The Old Testament, as now divided, is classified into four major divisions.

The Law. The five books written by Moses (Genesis, Exodus, Leviticus, Numbers, and Deuteronomy) are the foundation of the first covenant. In these books are the 613 commandments given at Mount Sinai, the Tabernacle form of worship, and the founding of the nation of Israel.

The History. The next twelve books, Joshua to

Esther, contain the entire story of the rest of the Old Testament. This is a history of the nation of Israel. Joshua records the conquest of the Promised Land in about the fifteenth century B.C.; Judges covers about 350 years of history during the rule of fifteen judges, such as Gideon and Samson. Then follows the reign of the kings (Saul, David, and Solomon) and the history of the divided kingdom through twenty-two kings each, over Israel and Judah, until the Babylonian captivity. Ezra and Nehemiah tell of the return from exile and the restoration of the nation, Nehemiah being the last book written before the 400 silent years separating the Testaments.

The Writings. These are usually called the Books of Poetry, or sometimes the Books of Wisdom. They are five books of inspirational reading, including the collection of songs (Psalms), Proverbs, and the Book of Job.

The Prophets. These seventeen books, Isaiah through Malachi, were written by prophets or preachers. They are sometimes divided into the five major prophets and twelve minor prophets. The words major and minor do not refer to their importance, but rather to the size of the books; the first five are larger and the next twelve are smaller or shorter books.

Classification of New Testament Books

The New Testament is likewise classified into four groups.

The Gospels. The first four books are the Gospels: Matthew, Mark, Luke and John. Here is the story of the life and ministry of Jesus Christ. The word *gospel* means "good news." The first three Gospels (Matthew, Mark and Luke) are also known as the *synoptic* Gospels, because they overlap and cover much of the same events. Thus many of the events, miracles, or parables found in one of these three Gospels will also be repeated in one or both of the others.

It is interesting to compare the styles of the four Gospels. Matthew wrote to a Jewish audience, picturing Jesus as the Messiah or "King," and often emphasized the fulfillment of Old Testament prophecies concerning Christ. Mark wrote for the Roman audience, picturing Christ as "Servant"; his Gospel is fast-moving, practical, and emphasizes miracles. Luke wrote for the Greek mind, picturing Jesus as the "Son of Man," writing with historical detail and emphasizing the parables of Jesus. John's Gospel is unique, covering much information not mentioned in the other three; he wrote to the world, presenting Jesus as the Son of God, defending His deity and emphasizing His doctrine and teachings.

Church History. The Acts of the Apostles stands alone in the New Testament as the history of the church. This is the only book describing the founding of the church on the Day of Pentecost and its early history and growth. The second half of the book follows the Apostle Paul on his missionary journeys as he established churches throughout the Gentile world.

The Book of Acts is unique in that it is the only book in the Bible giving instances of converts being saved. Only in this book are examples of anyone being baptized into the church and receiving the gift of the Holy Ghost. Anyone wanting to know the plan of salvation will always need to consult the Book of Acts to find the pattern in the Scriptures.

The Epistles. Commencing with the Book of Romans are letters written to saints and churches already established. Thus the epistles contain much instruction to the children of God on how to live a victorious Christian life and how to grow in the

Lord. They also contain instructions for the church concerning worship and discipline.

Since the Epistles are written to saints already saved, it is not surprising that we find very little reference to the plan of salvation. There is not a single example of anyone being baptized or receiving the Holy Ghost in the epistles—they had already experienced salvation.

The Epistles are sometimes divided into two groups: the fourteen Pauline Epistles that were written by the Apostle Paul and, secondly, the seven General Epistles written by others. The Pauline Epistles carry the name of the person or church to which they were sent; the General Epistles (addressed to the church as a whole) bear the name of their writer. The General Epistles were written by James, Peter, John, and Jude.

Prophecy. The Book of the Revelation can also be considered an epistle, but its subject matter places it into a class of its own. Revelation records the visions given to John on the Isle of Patmos, and is full of symbolic language dealing with things to come.

The above information on the divisions of the books may seem like very basic knowledge, yet it is probably some of the most important information a person will ever learn about the Bible. Otherwise how would he know where to look to find anything in the Scriptures?

Consider the subject of *salvation.* Suppose a Christian were witnessing or discussing the Scriptures with his friends. If they were to answer by quoting passages of Scripture about being saved such as those from Ephesians 2, "by grace are ye saved...not of works..." or Romans 10, "confess with thy mouth...and...believe in thine heart..." and "whosoever shall call upon the name of the Lord shall be saved" or I John 3, "We know that we have passed from death unto life, because we love the brethren" or I Corinthians 12, "do all speak with tongues?" The person may want to remind them that they are quoting epistles and that the epistles were written to those already converted. Everyone to whom the Epistles were addressed had already been baptized in Jesus' name and had all received the Holy Ghost, speaking with other tongues as the Spirit gave utterance.

If someone wants to find examples of converts being saved, he should read the Book of Acts. When a person wants to quote Ephesians (an epistle) about being saved, he should turn back to where the Ephesian church was established as recorded in Acts 19; there the Ephesians were baptized and received the Holy Ghost (Acts 19:5-6).

If a person wants to study the commandments, he should look in the Law division. If he desires to find the miracles of Jesus, he would look in the Gospels. If he wants verses of Scripture on baptism or salvation, he needs to look in the Book of Acts. The Christian who wants to find out how to overcome the world and grow in Christ needs to study the Epistles. For wisdom and inspiration, a person may look to the books of Poetry.

The Chronological Order

It is obvious by now that the books of the Bible are not arranged chronologically. For this reason it is profitable to consider the time of writing when reading a passage of Scripture.

Job was the first book written and is probably one of the oldest pieces of literature in existence. It dates back to the days of the patriarchs, possibly around the time Abraham left the land of the Chaldeans, one of the cradles of civilization.

The writings of Moses were next in chronological order. The Book of Genesis gives a history from creation through pre-historic eras; it provides the setting for the Exodus. The Books of Exodus through Deuteronomy reveal the covenant, the Law given at Mount Sinai, approximately 1500 B.C.

Next the historical books carry the story of Israel through Joshua, Judges, I and II Samuel, and I and II Kings with some overlapping by I and II Chronicles. The rest of the books of the Old Testament overlap and are contemporary with the historical books.

Some of the Psalms were written and compiled by David, whose story is told in II Samuel. Most of the Proverbs were written by Solomon, who is in I Kings. The writings of the prophets also paralleled their mention in the books of I and II Kings and II Chronicles; thus Isaiah, Hosea, Amos, Micah, Jeremiah and other prophets overlap those books.

Ezekiel and Daniel prophesied during the time of the Babylonian captivity in the sixth century B.C.

Ezra and Nehemiah described the history of the return of the Jews from exile. The Book of Esther, along with three prophets—Haggai, Zechariah, and Malachi—are contemporary with these two books. Malachi and Nehemiah are the last books of the Old Testament, written about 400 B.C.

The New Testament was mostly written by the apostles shortly after the ministry of Jesus Christ and while the events of the Apostolic Church were still happening. It is important to realize that the authors of the New Testament were eyewitnesses and participants in the events they described. The rumor that the New Testament was written by a later generation from oral legends passed down is false.

The Epistles of Paul overlap the Acts of the Apostles. On his second missionary journey, described in Acts 16-18, Paul wrote I and II Thessalonians to the church he had recently established at

Thessalonica. On the third missionary journey, described in Acts 19-21, Paul wrote I and II Corinthians, Romans, possibly Galatians, and his prison epistles (Ephesians, Colossians, Philippians, and Philemon). The prison epistles are so-called because Paul wrote them while imprisoned in Rome. It is also interesting to note that Paul's first nine epistles were addressed to churches, and his last four epistles, written later in his ministry, were addressed to the preachers or pastors. (This does not include the Hebrew letter which most attribute to Paul.) Thus these latter epistles, I and II Timothy, Titus, and Philemon, are also called the pastoral epistles.

Most or all of the apostles were martyred within a few years of each other, about thirty to forty years after Pentecost, with the exception of the Apostle John. He outlived the other apostles by another thirty years, dying a natural death around A.D. 100. Near the end of his life, John added the final touch that completed the Bible. John wrote not only his Gospel, but the three General Epistles bearing his name and the Book of the Revelation.

Thus was the end of the first century, the close of the Apostolic age, which closed the canon of the holy Scriptures. At least 1,600 years—maybe more, if we could put a date on the Book of Job—were spanned by the writing of the Bible.

The Time-Line

The message from Genesis to Revelation goes from the creation to the final judgment, from eternity to eternity.

We often use the word *dispensation* to describe a period of time in which God deals with man in a specific pattern. The Bible describes several dispensations.

The first days of man in the Garden of Eden was

the dispensation of Innocence. Then from Eden, approximately 4000 B.C., to the Flood was another dispensation; from the Flood to the call of Abraham was yet another. These three dispensations, covering approximately the first 2000 years of mankind, are summed up in the first eleven chapters of Genesis. At that point, the flow of the Scriptures slowed down, and the next thirty-nine chapters recounted the history of four generations. This era beginning with Abraham was the dispensation of the Patriarchs.

Beginning with Moses, 1500 B.C., was the dispensation of Law which covered the entire Old Testament except for the Book of Genesis.

The New Testament opened the church age, or the dispensation of Grace, which continues today. This dispensation will end with the Second Coming of Christ, an event the church believes to be very soon. Following this dispensation shall come the Kingdom Age, the Millennial dispensation, prophesied to be a thousand years of peace. These seven dispensations add up to about 7,000 years of history for mankind.

A serious student of the Bible would do well to draw a time line or a chart to map out the Scriptures as he studies his Bible. On this chart the major events and characters of the Bible can be mapped out in their order.

Amazing Unity

The Bible is a library of sixty-six separate books on religion, history, and philosophy; yet it is a single book. The Bible is "*the* Book." Although God is the true author, the Bible has at least forty writers of various backgrounds, writing in various styles over 1600 years of history. No other such collection of literature could be compared to this Book, for the

Bible retains a singular message and is without contradiction. It certainly is an amazing book. The smartest men in the world could never produce anything like it. It has to be a divine, God-breathed Book.

Test Your Knowledge

1. The key to "rightly dividing the Word of Truth" is simply knowing how the Bible is _____.

2. There are _____ books in the Old Testament, and _____ books in the New Testament.

3. The oldest book (written first) is _____.

4. The New Testament was completed by the year A.D. _____.

5. The Old Testament has four divisions. Name them and tell what books are included:

_____,
_____,
_____,
_____.

6. The New Testament has four divisions. Name them, and tell what books are included:

_____,
_____,
_____,
_____.

7. The plan of salvation is found in what book? _____

8. The life of Jesus Christ is found in _____.

9. The Epistles are _____ written to _____ and _____.

10. Are the books of the Bible in chronological order? _____

Apply Your Knowledge

Make eight sheets of paper, the size of your Bible pages, and insert these sheets into your Bible at the beginning of each division. Write on each sheet the title of that division, along with any other pertinent information you may want to include (for instance: a description of the unique points of that division, a time-line chart, or a list of main events and characters).

Leave these sheets in your Bible for a few weeks. As you use your Bible with these sheets in it, you will become familiar with the overall picture of its layout.

Expand Your Knowledge

If you have not already done so, why not memorize all sixty-six books of the Bible this week. If this sounds like an impossible task, you will be surprised at how easy it can be if you will group the books into their topical divisions. And use your fingers! Look at the five fingers of your hand and count, as you touch each finger, 5-12-5-5-12. That is the number of Old Testament books in each division when you divide the Prophets into major and minor. As you touch each finger, remember: five law, twelve history, five writings (or poetry), five major prophets, twelve minor prophets. Then it will be easy to memorize one division at a time. First memorize only the five books of the law, then the twelve books of history. Continue in this same fashion.

The same can be done for the New Testament. Again looking at your five fingers, remember 4-1-14-7-1. That represents four Gospels, one history (Acts), fourteen Pauline Epistles, seven General Epistles, and one prophecy (Revelation). You can memorize the whole list this week!

The Complete Word 4

> *"For I testify unto every man that heareth the words of the prophecy of this book, If any man shall add unto these things, God shall add unto him the plagues that are written in this book: And if any man shall take away from the words of the book of this prophecy, God shall take away his part out of the book of life, and out of the holy city, and from the things which are written in this book."*
>
> *Revelation 22:18-19*

Start with the Scriptures

Exodus 31:18
Deuteronomy 17:18; 31:24-26
I Samuel 10:25
I Corinthians 3:10-11; 14:37

Galatians 1:8-9
Ephesians 2:20
Colossians 4:16
II Peter 3:15-16

Can we trust our Bible to be the *whole* truth, the *complete* Word of God? This chapter will build our confidence that the Bible has been given to us accurate and complete. There are no lost books, additions or deletions; nothing has been rewritten, revised, or changed by man.

Anyone familiar with Roman Catholic tradition knows that with them the question of the canon is very much alive. Catholics claim that their early church councils determined what the Bible was, that it is a Catholic book, and other churches do not have all the books in their Bibles. This simply is not true.

The Bible was the Word of God long before any Catholic church council ever convened. The inspiration and authority of the Scriptures was determined by God; man can only recognize and accept what God has already inspired.

The word canon (originally "a reed") means "a rule of standard for measuring." Since the fourth century the word *canon* has been used to refer to a list of the accepted books, recognized as the genuine Scriptures.

Canonicity is determined by God. A book is called canonical because it is inspired and placed in the Bible by God. When the Scriptures were written, they immediately possessed absolute authority; they did not need for men to pass judgment and decide whether to place them in the Bible.

The Old Testament Canon

At Mount Sinai the Lord presented to Moses two tables of stone "written with the finger of God" (Exodus 31:18). On a second trip up the mountain after the first stones were broken, Moses hewed out two more tables of stone and again the Lord wrote upon them His Commandments (Exodus 34:1). And for forty days on the mountain, the Lord dictated to Moses additional laws; "The LORD said unto Moses, Write thou these words. . ." (Exodus 34:27-28). The Word of God was immediately accepted. "And all the people answered with one voice, and said, All the words which the LORD hath said will we do. And Moses wrote all the words of the LORD. . ." (Exodus 24:3-4).

From the beginning, the Levitical priesthood (the ministry) was the guardian of the canon. "When Moses had made an end of writing the words of this law in a book, until they were finished, That Moses commanded the Levites. . .saying, Take this book of the law, and put it in the side of the ark of the covenant of the LORD your God, that it may be there for a witness against thee" (Deuteronomy 31:24-26). Thus the ark of the covenant in the Holy of Holies of the Tabernacle (and later the Temple) became the depository for the official holy books.

The stone tablets from Mount Sinai were placed in the ark (Exodus 40:20; Deuteronomy 10:2, 5). The Book of Deuteronomy was placed there (Deuteronomy 31:24-26). As other books were written, they were also placed there.

These tablets and scrolls kept in the Tabernacle were the originals from which all copies were to be made. According to Deuteronomy 17, every king was to have his own personal copy of the Law and this copy was to be made from the official books kept by the priests (Deuteronomy 17:18).

Daniel carried the holy books into exile in 606 B.C. (Daniel 9:2) before the Babylonians destroyed the first Temple. This exile had a profound effect on Jewish consciousness of their holy books, and scribes (as Ezra) arose to help preserve the sacred collection of scrolls.

After the destruction of the last Temple (A.D. 70) and the scattering of the Jews, there was no longer a functioning priesthood to control the official canon. Leading rabbis obtained Rome's permission to reconstitute the Sanhedrin on a spiritual basis. Their Council at Jamnia (A.D. 90) was the first authoritative discussion of the Hebrew canon outside the priesthood. They considered all challenges, but the list remained unchanged.

A Progressive Canon

As mentioned in the last chapter, the Old Testament was originally divided into two sections, the Law and the Prophets. The Law was in five scrolls. The Prophets were in seventeen more scrolls (nineteen books). The minor prophets were all one scroll and Jews still consider it one book called "The Twelve." Ezra and Nehemiah were one scroll. Four scrolls—Joshua, Judges, Samuel, and Kings—were grouped together as the "former prophets." Ruth was part of the scroll of Judges; Lamentations was at the end of Jeremiah.

The prophets progressively added these seventeen scrolls to the canon as they were written over a period of 1,000 years. A prophet is anyone who speaks for God, but to add to sacred writ, some believe that a prophet had to be recognized by the priesthood and enrolled in the register of the Temple. (See Ezekiel 13:9.)

Qualified and inspired prophets sometimes completed the previous scroll before starting a new book. This explains how the deaths of Moses and of Joshua were added as additional chapters to the books written by them, or how the genealogy of Ruth's descendants could be added years later to the Book of Ruth, and why there are some passages repeated more than once in the Scriptures. For example, the last two verses of II Chronicles are the first two verses of Ezra, and some chapters in Kings are repeated in Isaiah and Jeremiah. In other words, the prophets recorded a continuous sacred history, tying their books together into a canonical unit.

Chronicles gives a number of examples of how the prophets worked together gradually developing the canon. For instance, the history of David was written by Samuel, Nathan, and Gad (I Chronicles 29:29); the history of Solomon was recorded by Ahijah, Nathan, and Iddo (II Chronicles 9:29); the history of Rehoboam was recorded by Shemaiah and Iddo (II Chronicles 12:15); Jehoshaphat's story was recorded by Jehu (II Chronicles 20:34); Hezekiah's story was written by Isaiah (II Chronicles 32:32).

Another evidence of this progressive canon is the way that writers referred to or quoted previously recorded Scriptures, thus recognizing the authority of preceding prophets. Ezekiel referred to Job (Ezekiel 14:14, 20), the Book of Judges refers to Joshua, I Kings mentions David's story told in I and II Samuel. Dozens of examples could be compiled.

Completion of the Old Testament

Eventually the prophetic unction ceased and the Old Testament canon was complete. Some scholars feel that the end of the Old Testament prophetic era was prophesied in such passages as Zechariah 13:2-5. The New Testament, which refers to or quotes hundreds of Old Testament verses of Scripture, never quoted anything written after Malachi. Jesus used the expression "From the blood of Abel unto the blood of Zacharias" (Luke 11:51) whose death is described in II Chronicles 24:21, the last book in the order of the old Hebrew canon; this would be the same to us as saying "from Genesis to Malachi."

That the Old Testament prophetic ministry ceased and the canon ended is also testified to by many secular witnesses such as the Dead Sea Scrolls and the Maccabees. The Babylonian Talmud stated "after Malachi the Holy Spirit departed from Israel." Other talmudic statements refer to the end of the Old Testament: "Up to this point the prophets prophesied through the Holy Spirit; from this time onward incline thine ear and listen to the sayings of the wise" (Seder Olam Rabba 30); "The books of Ben Sira and whatever books have been written since his time are not canonical" (Tosefta Yadaim 3:5).

Josephus referred to books written after the close of the Old Testament, but they were not "deemed worthy of like credit with what preceded, because the exact succession of the prophets ceased. But what faith we have placed in our own writings is evident by our conduct; for though so long a time has now passed, no one has dared to add anything to them or to take anything from them or to alter anything in them." The Old Testament was complete.

There are many other religious and historical books of interest, as well as some imaginative spurious books with false claims. But God did not place them in the Bible; and neither should we. Just because they discuss religious people does not make them inspired Scriptures.

The Bible itself refers to books that are not canonical. Jude 14 quoted I Enoch 1:9; Apostle Paul quoted the pagan philosopher, Aratus (Acts 17:28); and Epimenides (Titus 1:12). Jesus quoted a non-canonical espousal ceremony (John 14:2-3). Joshua 10:13 and II Samuel 1:18 refer to the Book of Jasher, and the Book of the wars of the Lord is mentioned in Numbers 21:14. Nestle lists 132 allusions to non-canonical books in his Greek New Testament. But these books are not "lost" books of the Bible; they never were part of it.

The Apocrypha

The greatest questions arise concerning the Apocrypha. Why did the Catholic church add it to their Bible in A.D. 1546?

The earliest evidence of the Apocrypha is a fourth century manuscript of the Septuagint containing fifteen additional books (eighteen in later editions) although they were never part of the Hebrew Scriptures. Soon after, the Armenian church added these books to their Syriac translation. Earlier Syrian Bibles, like the second century Peshitta translation, did not include them. They were added to the Latin Vulgate after Jerome's death because Jerome rejected them and strongly protested their use.

Supporters of the Apocrypha also claim that some Catholic "fathers" as Tertullian in the third century and Augustine in the fourth century spoke with high regard for these books and said they were read in churches; but other "fathers" as Origen and Cyril, spoke strongly against them.

The Roman Catholic church turned to these Apocryphal books as a reaction to the Protestant Reformation. The counter-reformation Council of Trent, A.D. 1546, formally accepted seven of the Apocryphal books and added them to the Catholic Bibles. Five more short sections were also added as additional verses to Esther and Daniel. The other books of the Apocrypha were rejected altogether. The Greek Orthodox church accepted the Apocrypha in their synods beginning in A.D. 1638 although many of their scholars continued to reject them, and their catechism of 1839 still specifically rejected them as not part of the original Scriptures.

The Catholic Douay version of the Bible contains these seven Apocryphal books: I and II Maccabees, Tobit, Judith, Wisdom of Solomon, Ecclesiasticus, and Baruch, plus additional verses in Esther and Daniel. (The rejected books include I and II Esdras, Manasseh, III and IV Maccabees and Psalm 151.)

Although these books, mostly written from 200 B.C. to A.D. 100, may be interesting historically, they should not be accepted as Scripture. We reject the Apocrypha for the following reasons:

The Apocryphal books themselves nowhere claim to be inspired words of God. In fact several passages in them specifically disclaim inspiration and speak of the day of the prophets as having ceased (I Maccabees 14:41, II Baruch 85:3, and Prologues to Judith and Ecclesiasticus).

The Jews never accepted them as part of the Old Testament. Even secular scholars, as Josephus and Philo, rejected them specifically as never a part of the Palestinian Canon.

Jesus never once quoted from nor referred to them.

The New Testament, which quotes hundreds of Old Testament passages, never once mentions the Apocrypha and never quotes anything written after Malachi.

The Early Church, and the apostles ignored the Apocrypha.

Churches, like the Roman Catholics and Greek Orthodox, that today include the Apocrypha, did not do so in their earlier history.

The Apocryphal books contain heretical, fanciful, fictitious tales and even immoral teachings. For instance, the fanciful tales of Bel and the Dragon, the fictitious legend of Susanna, and other unscriptural tales are devoid of any hint of inspiration. The fictional novel, Judith, supports lying and situation ethics, and II Maccabees contains false doctrine—praying for the dead.

These books are also full of historical, geographical, and chronological errors.

The New Testament Canon

The basis of the New Testament is the apostolic ministry. "Whatsoever thou shalt bind on earth shall be bound in heaven," (Matthew 16:19) and since Pentecost the church "continued stedfastly in the apostles' doctrine" (Acts 2:42). The apostles were ordained and commissioned to write the New Testament.

As the test of Old Testament Scriptures was their prophetic authorship, the test of the New Testament was its apostolic authority. "And are built upon the foundation of the apostles and prophets, Jesus Christ himself being the chief cornerstone" (Ephesians 2:20). All Scriptures were written by either a prophet (Old Testament) or an apostle (New Testament). The Apostle Paul told the Corinthians, "I have laid the foundation. . .let every man take heed how he buildeth thereupon. For other foundation can no man lay. . ." (I Corinthians 3:10-11).

Did the apostles realize they were writing Scripture? Yes. "If any man think himself to be a prophet, or spiritual, let him acknowledge that the things that I write unto you are the commandments of the Lord" (I Corinthians 14:37). (Also see II Corinthians 1:13.) And again in Ephesians 3:1-5, Paul related that they were reading the "dispensation of the grace of God. . .given me to you-ward: How that by revelation he [God] made known unto me the mystery. . .as it is now revealed unto his holy apostles and prophets by the Spirit."

Apostolic authority was final. Paul wrote, "But though we, or an angel from heaven, preach any other gospel unto you than that which we have preached unto you, let him be accursed. As we said before, so say I now again, If any man preach any other gospel unto you than that ye have received, let him be accursed" (Galatians 1:8-9).

But as years pass, who is to determine whether a doctrine was apostolic or not? What did Jesus really teach? The written record by eyewitnesses, the apostles themselves, provided our permanent written deposit of truth. "God, who. . .spake in time past unto the fathers by the prophets, Hath in these last days spoken unto us by his Son. . .and was confirmed unto us by them that heard him; God also bearing them witness, both with signs and wonders. . ." (Hebrews 1:1-2 and 2:3-4). The writings of the apostles were automatically accepted as sacred; if the apostles wrote it, it was assumed that no other test of canonicity was needed.

This high regard for the word of the apostles continued even after their death. As you read the historical writings of early centuries such as Ignatius, Clement, Polycarp, Justin Martyr, and Irenaius, there is a constant appeal to the apostles. Doctrinal questions were answered by "The apostles taught..." or "This came down to us from the apostles"; these phrases occur repeatedly in early church history and literature of the Ante-Nicene fathers.

Progressive Canonization of the New Testament

Apostolic epistles received by churches were accepted immediately, copied and exchanged with other churches. "When this epistle is read among you, cause that it be read also in the church of the Laodiceans; and that ye likewise read the epistle from Laodicea." The epistle from Laodicea is thought by scholars to be the Book of Ephesians or Philemon. Peter refers to Paul's epistles and equates them with "the other scriptures" (II Peter 3:15-16).

The New Testament was written by the apostles and circulated during their lifetime. We must reject the modernist claim that legends were passed down orally to succeeding generations and finally recorded many years later by others. This is simply not true.

Close of the Canon

With the death of the Apostle John and his writing the Revelation came the completion of the New Testament. The canon of the Scriptures is forever closed. The Bible is complete and "For ever, O LORD, thy word is settled in heaven" (Psalm

119:89).

The Book of Revelation closes with this final warning, "For I testify unto every man that heareth the words of the prophecy of this book, If any man shall add unto these things, God shall add unto him the plagues that are written in this book: And if any man shall take away from the words of the book of this prophecy, God shall take away his part out of the book of life, and out of the holy city, and from the things which are written in this book" (Revelation 22:18-19).

Recognizing the Canon

It was a heretic, Marcion (A.D. 140) that inspired the first listing of canonical books of the New Testament. Because he did not like the Apostle Paul, Marcion had circulated a list of only ten books that he accepted as Scripture, rejecting all others. As a reaction to this heretical step, many early churches began to share lists of the scrolls they had in their possession to see if their collection was complete.

Three things caused discussions to arise in the early centuries about which books were apostolic and thus canonical.

- Reaction to the heretic Marcion.
- Persecution by Rome of those possessing Christian Scripture.
- The development of the *codex,* a form of manuscript on separate sheets to be bound into a book instead of a scroll, allowing the collection of many apostolic scrolls to be combined into one collection.

However, there is plenty of evidence from even the second century (Muratorian Canon, Codex Barococcio, Syriac and Latin translations, and quotes from the early "fathers") that our New Testament is identical to that accepted from the beginning. There was never a serious question about any of the twenty-seven books we have today.

The Council of Hippo and Synod of Carthage addressed the subject of which books were canonical and their lists, like Athanasius' is exactly as we have it today. The fact that several early church councils discussed the canon and listed books does not mean that they decided or invented the Bible. At best they only ratified what had been commonly accepted long before. As one historian said, "The Bible is not an authorized collection of books, but a collection of authorized books."

The main value of various church councils' pronouncements on the canon was not in listing the accepted books, but in eliminating those books not listed. This prevented illegitimate books from being inserted.

Other Literature

Just as libraries are filled with books by modern authors, the Early Church also produced much literature besides the Bible. The Epistle of Barnabas, the Epistle of Clement, and the Shepherd of Hermas are some of the works that interest scholars because these popular books were read by first century churches in apostolic days. Though these early books are interesting historically, we must remember that they are not a part of the Scriptures—nor were they ever accepted as such.

The second and third centuries also produced much literature, including books by heretical gnostics, pagans and even fanciful legends forged over apostolic names in later centuries. Though these never had a claim to being part of Holy Scripture, we should be aware of their existence.

Even certain cults continue trying to add their writings to the Scriptures. The Book of Mormon is one example. But all such writings should be firmly rejected. The sixty-six books of the Bible are the complete written Word of God. The Canon is closed. No person should add to or take from that which is written.

Test Your Knowledge

1. The guardian of the Old Testament canon was the _____.
2. The source of the New Testament was the _____.
3. The official Old Testament holy books were kept in _____.
4. List several reasons for rejecting the Apocrypha.

Apply Your Knowledge

What did the apostles teach? Choose any doctrine or subject and prepare to search through your Bible. Answer this question about your chosen subject: "What did the apostles teach concerning this subject?"

Expand Your Knowledge

The next chapter covers how the Bible has been preserved through the ages. In preparation for the chapter, define the following words, using a reliable dictionary such as Webster's:
Canon—
Inspiration—
Cuneiform—
Hieroglyphic—
Study the Scriptures for the following chapter before reading the chapter.

5. Preserving the Word

"For ever, O LORD, thy word is settled in heaven."
Psalm 119:89

Start with the Scriptures

Jeremiah 36:21-32
Psalm 12:6-7

Matthew 5:17-18
II Timothy 4:13

Two to three thousand years of transmitting, copying, and preserving separate us from the time of the original writing of the Scriptures. Has the Bible suffered in the process? No! We can confidently reject the charge of unlearned critics that it is full of mistakes and changes.

Our assurance of reliability can be illustrated by comparing a modern text with the Dead Sea Scrolls. These ancient scrolls found in caves near the Dead Sea in 1947, perhaps the greatest archeological manuscript discovery in history, are fully one thousand years older than the previously known ninth or tenth century Massoretic manuscripts. Let us compare the evidence.

R. Laird Harris in *Inspiration and Canonicity of the Bible* illustrated a side by side comparison of Isaiah 53. The modern Hebrew text of 166 words contained 17 letters or marks that were different in the Dead Sea scroll from Qumran cave one. Of these 17 letters, ten were simple changes in spelling of the same word due to modern language; four were stylistic changes of conjunctions, again due to language changes. Only three letters making one word ("light" in verse 11) were missing from this Qumran scroll. And this word has support in that it is found in other manuscripts (including the Septuagint). After 2000 years, it still says exactly the same thing! The Bible is reliable!

Why Write?

God could have spoken directly in each age or allowed oral traditions to pass by word of mouth to successive generations, but the "more excellent way" was to immortalize His Word in a permanent record, "a more sure word of prophecy" (II Peter 1:19). This permanence has several advantages.

Preservation. A permanent record overcomes the disadvantages of failing memories and the chance of accidental corruption, repeating what we have heard. Oral repetition has a way of evolving and embellishing the story; this can be observed by whispering a story from one person to the next around a circle and seeing how the story ends.

Precision. Writing is specific and exact. To express oneself accurately in writing requires much more understanding than simply speaking.

Propagation. A recorded medium allows mass

dissemination to anyone anytime without depending on momentary "word of mouth," personal encounters.

God still speaks today. The gifts of prophecy, tongues and interpretation still grace the church; dreams, visions and revelations are yet possible. But none of these can supersede nor replace the written Word of God. Any present day message from God should be tested. When someone claims God told or showed him something contrary to the written Word, we should choose to hold fast to that which is written. Heaven and earth may pass away but God's Word stands forever.

The Invention of Writing

The Bible began when written language began.

In the first 300 years after the Flood, God's judgment at the tower of Babel brought different languages and a scattering of the people. Abram (Abraham) moved from Ur to Haran. There Abraham wrote his language (Akkadian) by picture drawings. These pictograms eventually developed into the wedged shaped *cuneiform* script that was commonly impressed into the clay tablets of Sumar and Mesopotamia.

Jacob followed his son Joseph to carry the chosen tribe down into Egypt. (Abraham visited here also.) Here pictograms reached their most advanced stage in *hieroglyphic* writing. Yet Egyptian hieroglyphics, as advanced as it was, had major drawbacks. (1) A picture represented a whole word; thus hundreds and thousands of symbols would need to be memorized for even the simplest communication. (2) The precision of making the pictures exact would be very critical. (3) And again, a symbol had an expanding number of meanings. For instance, a circle represented the sun but could also convey the idea of day, or light, or heat, and later was also used phonetically as a syllable of a word of unrelated meaning that had a similar sound. A picture of a bee could also mean honey, sweetness, or even busy activity. If the people of the world were ever going to communicate, they would need an alphabet based on sounds of words.

The alphabet (according to *World Book Encyclopedia*) was invented by Seirites (Semites) on the Sinai peninsula around 1800 to 1500 B.C. The Phoenicians perfected it into 22 symbols for sounds—the world's first alphabet. Canaanite, Syric, Aramaic, Moabitic and other Syro-Palestinian languages (including Hebrew) readily adopted this alphabet. The door to written expression was thrown open for the first time in history.

Why was the Law given at Mount Sinai? It was no coincidence that God led Moses out of Egypt, across the Red Sea, and to Mount Sinai. This area of the world had been the very birthplace of the alphabet, and the Law was given soon after its invention.

God wrote first, carving the Commandments into the stone tablets at Sinai. Then the Lord commanded Moses, "Write thou these words..." (Exodus 34:27) and again, "Write this for a memorial in a book..." (Exodus 17:14). Many others were also commanded to write the words of God which He desired to communicate to His people. In fact, over 450 times the Bible refers to writing the Scriptures.

```
× w ʮ φ r ] ° ∓ ʮ y ( y Z ⊕ H ⊥ Y ∃ ⊲ ﬧ ﬞ †
```

T S R Q - P O X N M L K I - H Z F E D C B A

This illustration (above) is the Hebrew alphabet used throughout the Old Testament times. It was only at the end of Old Testament times that the more modern Hebrew square script began to replace the old Semitic form.

About the 10th century B.C., the Greeks borrowed the Phoenician alphabet, made a few revisions and added vowels to form the Greek alphabet. From the Greek came all our popular modern scripts, including the Cyrillic alphabet (used in Russia today) and the Latin alphabet used in English and other European languages.

Writing was, at first, right to left; later it went from right to left and back (like plowing a field back and forth). Ancient writing was with all capitals (uncial) with no space between words or sentences and no punctuation, and the pre-Greek alphabets did not include vowel sounds.

Writing Materials

Papyrus, made in Egypt from strips of reeds pressed into a paper-like mat, served as the major writing material for many centuries. Sheets of it could be bound together into a long roll or scroll. A book of the Bible could be written on a scroll of fifteen, thirty, or maybe forty feet long.

Other writing materials included clay tablets (Ezekiel 4:1), especially in Syria and Mesopotamia, stone carvings, and pottery (ostraca). Archeologists learn much from ostraca, potsherds or fragments of broken jugs and pottery vessels used by common people for writing.

After 190 B.C., parchment came into more extensive use (after Pergamos in Asia Minor began promoting it). Parchment and vellum are made from animal skins, treated in lime, stretched, scraped and chalked.

The Chinese invention of paper did not enter the Western world until the European crusades against the Moslems in the late 1100's. Even then paper was handmade from rag pulp until the 19th century industrial revolution introduced machines that could mass produce paper from chemically treated wood pulp.

A Great Invention

Johannes Gutenberg's movable type printing press (invented around 1440-1450) is often proclaimed the most important invention in the world. This one great leap forward in communication was the foundation for the Reformation, the Renaissance, the industrial revolution, and the modern age of science.

The first book printed was a Latin Bible. Gutenberg needed a whole day to set type for each page, and the press reached a maximum speed of ten sheets per hour. It took two years to produce 150 copies of the first edition of a printed Bible. Although terribly slow by today's standards, it was an incredible improvement over hand-copying manuscripts.

Guarding the Sacred Trust

Jewish scribes had such high regard for sacred Scripture that when a manuscript began to show signs of wear, it was removed from official circulation and reverently disposed of, stored in special library cabinets (*genizah*). When these holy *genizah* were full, the manuscripts would be buried or disposed of with an elaborate "funeral" ceremony. Such sacred treasures were not allowed to fall into "unclean" hands.

The preparing of a new manuscript could take years. A scribe of the old Talmudic order, under strict professional rules, would not begin his tedious task each day until he performed his morning prayers, bathed, and was in full Jewish ceremonial dress. Notice some of his Talmudic rules:

(1) He could use only special quality parchment from "clean" animals and ink made by a specific "kosher" recipe.

(2) Each sheet would be first ruled with exact guidelines, a certain number of columns all identical, no more than thirty letters wide and no less than forty-eight wide, and no more than sixty lines long. Each page was planned ahead so that the last word at the end of the Torah ended exactly at the end of the last line.

(3) Lettering had exact rules on shape and spacing with no two letters touching, and spacing measured by the number of hairs.

(4) Not a single letter, not even a *yod,* was to be written from memory. Every word was to be looked at and pronounced aloud before writing.

(5) To write the name of the Lord, the pen was to be first cleaned, the scribe consecrated, and he was not to respond to distraction while writing it even if addressed by a king.

(6) If more than three marks had to be corrected, the entire sheet of parchment was condemned; he had to start over. Corrections were not allowed after thirty days; if even one mistake was discovered in an existing manuscript it had to be destroyed to prevent its use.

(7) At the end of each sheet, every word and every letter was methodically counted.

After the 5th century, the Massoretic tradition governed the scribe's trade even more strictly. A Massorete worked only in the presence of proofreaders that checked each word before proceeding. Such exacting regulations meant it could take up to fifteen years of tedious labor just preparing one Torah scroll. Massoretes revered the sacred writ so much that even an acknowledged error (by previous scribe) would not be corrected in the text but only noted in the margin.

These scribes were masters of trivia. They counted the number of words and letters and could tell you the exact middle word or middle letter in each book; they numbered the times each letter of the alphabet occurred in each book. Such trivialities only reinforced the precision of their work.

Because a new manuscript was an exact duplicate equal to the one copied, and since age was no advantage, the old worn copy was destroyed. This explains why so few Hebrew manuscripts have survived to today.

The New Testament situation is just the opposite. Instead of a shortage, there is an overabundance of manuscripts. While the church would often have dedicated scribes make good quality copies of New Testament books, there was also a proliferation of inferior copies. The excitement of receiving an apostolic epistle and the desire to share it with other churches created a demand for many immediate copies. Eager young converts whose enthusiasm outran their skill hurriedly wrote out copies of their own.

Yet such excess had its own built-in safeguard. Though the autographs of the apostles and other New Testament workers were not preserved, (Perhaps that is so we would worship the God of the Word rather than idolize a relic of the Word itself), there are so many thousands of copies to compare that it is possible to detect and confront any errors.

Critics sometimes claim that over 200,000 variant readings in New Testament manuscripts prove the Bible is unreliable. This claim is misleading. Most claimed differences are in spelling of words; and if a differently spelled word appears in 3,000 copies of this manuscript, the critic counts that as 3,000 variants.

These, along with obvious mistakes which no

scholar would seriously consider, eliminate 99.8 percent of the critic's list. We are left with only 400 real variants buried in thousands of manuscripts, and only 50 of these have any significance, and none affect any doctrine. This is amazing accuracy!

The scrutiny of critics, rather than weakening the case for the Bible, only makes it infinitely stronger. Schaff quotes Scrivener: "We possess so many manuscripts and other evidences that we are never left in doubt on a single passage. It cannot be too strongly asserted the accuracy of the text far supersedes every other book in the world."

The Proven Word

The Bible is the best preserved book in the world with over 13,000 manuscripts of the New Testament (in whole or part) of which 5,000 manuscripts are in Greek. Of no other ancient writing do we possess so many manuscripts. The best attested work besides the Bible is Homer's *Iliad* of which 643 manuscripts exist (far short of the 13,000 of the New Testament), and 5 percent of the *Iliad* are variant readings.

Most great works of old came to us by only a few, sometimes only one manuscript. For instance, Aristotle is known by only five manuscripts, the oldest of which dates 1400 years after he lived. Plato's works exist in only seven manuscripts, the oldest dating 1200 years after his death. Herodotus is known by eight manuscripts, 1300 years removed. Caesar's Gallic Wars exists in only ten copies made 900 years after his death. Yet no classical scholar would dare argue the authenticity of any of these classics.

Sir Frederic Kenyon in *The Story of the Bible* stated, "It cannot be too strongly asserted that ...the text of the Bible is certain. The number of manuscripts (and other evidences) is so large that it is. . .certain that the true reading of every doubtful passage is preserved. . . .This can be said of no other ancient book in the world."

The Indestructible Word

King Jehoiakim of Judah so despised the Word, he sent Jehudi to fetch Jeremiah's scroll from the scribe's chambers. "And it came to pass, that when Jehudi had read three or four leaves, he cut it with the penknife, and cast it into the fire that was on the hearth, until all the roll was consumed in the fire that was on the hearth. Yet they were not afraid, nor rent their garments, neither the king, nor any of his servants that heard all these words" (Jeremiah 36:23-24).

God's judgment was pronounced on Jehoiakim and "Then took Jeremiah another roll, and gave it to Baruch the scribe, the son of Neriah; who wrote therein from the mouth of Jeremiah all the words of the book which Jehoiakim king of Judah had burned in the fire" (Jeremiah 36:32).

Imagine, using a knife to cut parts out of the Bible! Yet kings and armies often tried to destroy the Word. Antiochus Epiphanes invaded Jerusalem in 170 B.C., desecrating the Temple by sacrificing swine and erecting an idol of Zeus. His armies sought to destroy all of the sacred Scriptures; they burned all manuscripts they could find. This prompted the famed Maccabean revolt.

Roman persecutions of early Christians began with Nero (A.D. 64) when Paul and other apostles were among the martyrs. Over the next 200 years a series of persecutions saw hundreds of Christians thrown to lions, burned alive, or crucified. This climaxed about A.D. 300 in the most severe persecution of the Roman Empire. Yet in this, Emperor

Diocletian's major effort was against the Bible itself. Roman armies swept the countryside not only demolishing churches but specifically searching for Holy Scriptures, publicly burning every single page found.

It was said that some of the manuscripts were brought to Diocletian for him to personally burn to heat his bathwater. His edict against the Bible was so widespread that Rome was already planning a celebration (coins had already been minted) commemorating the empire's triumph over Christianity; announcements read that the church had been "blotted out and Christian superstition is destroyed." The historic irony is that the next Roman emperor, Constantine, commissioned Eusebius to prepare fifty manuscripts of the Bible at government expense.

Foxe's Book of Martyrs records the history of much of the severe persecution of the Inquisition when thousands were martyred, sometimes for as simple a crime as possessing a Bible.

The council of Toulouse in 1229 "forbade" anyone to possess a copy of the Bible (exception was made for authorized church officials). Even as late as 1559, Pope Paul IV's list of "forbidden books" included all vernacular (non-Latin) Bibles.

For years England vacillated between promoting and banning the Bible. King Henry VII (1530) signed a proclamation prohibiting the possession of the Scriptures in native languages, but ten years later required Bibles to be made available in all churches at a price of ten pennies. Then the following year (1541) he again forbade the printing of Bibles, followed by rules that men could read it only in private and women were forbidden access to it altogether.

Queen Mary began her rule in 1553, prohibiting by royal decree all public reading of the Bible and forbade publishing or importing it. Soldiers were dispatched to search print shops to insure none were being printed. Anyone caught concealing Bibles was beheaded or burned. Over 300 Englishmen were burned at the stake for possessing a Bible.

The German countryside was swept by the Thirty Years War (1618-1648), partly a religious Protestant/Catholic war. Spanish soldiers relentlessly searched out Bibles, and all copies of Scripture were seized and burned as soon as the invaders caught sight of them. Hundreds of thousands of Bibles, including many valuable old manuscripts, were destroyed.

No other book has been so attacked in mass, opposed with such venom and skepticism, denounced and criticized with such thoroughness—every line of it. A thousand times over, infidels have planned its funeral and inscribed its tombstone. But it is the infidels that occupy the tombs and the Bible lives on.

The famed French infidel, Voltaire (1778), prophesied that within 100 years Christianity would pass from existence and the Bible would lie unknown and forgotten. What irony that fifty years after Voltaire's death the Geneva Bible Society would use Voltaire's press in his own house to print stacks of new Bibles.

Test Your Knowledge

True or False

_____ 1. The discovery of the Dead Sea Scrolls was perhaps the most significant archeological discovery of this century.

_____ 2. God could have chosen to simply speak directly to each succeeding generation rather than to have recorded His Word.

_____ 3. Really, there is no significant advantage in having God's Word in written form.

_____ 4. Writing is specific and exact.

_____ 5. The Bible was begun many years after the invention of written language.

_____ 6. God Himself carved His commandments into the first stone tablets at Sinai.

_____ 7. Ancient writing included both upper and lower case letters.

_____ 8. One of the major forms of writing material during the times of the writing of the Bible was papyrus.

_____ 9. Paper was invented in Europe.

_____ 10. The Bible is the best preserved book in the world.

Applying Your Knowledge

Can you imagine copying an entire manuscript of the New Testament, not to mention the entire Bible? Realizing the expended effort of countless people to preserve the Word of God gives a person a much greater appreciation for it.

Choose a smaller Book of the New Testament or several chapters of a large one and copy it by hand. This can surely build your appreciation of the Scriptures as well as by edifying in learning that which is written. After doing this exercise, go back and check your work. Chances are you will find some mistakes. Imagine what painstaking care had to be taken to keep the Bible as free from error as possible.

Expand Your Knowledge

Using a Bible encyclopedia, study about the origin of various New Testament translations. It is amazing to consider that so many different translations have come forth from only a couple of basic Greek texts. This little exercise in study will prepare you for the following chapter.

Translating the Word 6

> *"But now is made manifest, and by the scriptures of the prophets, according to the commandment of the everlasting God, made known to all nations for the obedience of faith."*
>
> Romans 16:26

Start with the Scriptures

Deuteronomy 32:3
Isaiah 52:7
Jonah 3:7
Revelation 1:11
Psalm 68:11
Acts 8:30
Romans 10:18

The unique character of the Scriptures sets their entire existence apart from that of humanly conceived documents. Their uniqueness extends not just to the autographs (original writings) but to copies and translations. The gracious influence of God over His Word did not end when the original penman ceased his work; it extends even to our day.

It is certainly possible that a corrupt manuscript can be made and a poor translation rendered. Indeed, this has often been the case. But God has a sovereign manner of minimizing the influence of such tainted work, while maximizing the influence of His perfectly preserved and correctly translated Word.

If only the original manuscripts were inspired and without error and it be wrong to copy or translate the autographs, then we do not have the Word of God today. Few people at any point in history would have had access to the autographs. Probably not even the apostles ever saw the entirety of the infallible Scriptures, for at no time were the original manuscripts collected into one volume.

If only the untranslated Hebrew, Aramaic, and Greek form the inerrant Word, then few people will ever have access to the Word of God.

But it is abundantly testified in Scripture that the preserving influence of the Holy Spirit would extend to copies and translations. (See Psalm 12:6-7.) When Jesus commanded His disciples to go teach all nations, inherent in His command was the implication that His Words could be translated into the tongues of all people of all ages and still remain His Word.

Early History of Translations

The traditional date for the translation of the Septuagint is around 250 B.C. The work is said to have been done by seventy-two Jewish scholars in Alexandria, Egypt. This would place the Septuagint as the earliest translation of the Old Testament. There is some question as to the validity of this date, since this historical reconstruction rests upon such scant evidence, namely the so-called *Letter of Aristeas*. It has been suggested, with no little support, that the Septuagint is actually a post-Christian document.

At any rate, Jesus gave His approval to the Hebrew Scriptures in use at His time. Not once did He suggest that the current Scriptures were any less than the inerrant Word of God.

Archeological work done in the late 1940's at Masada unearthed copies of Old Testament books which could definitely be dated as prior to A.D. 70. In all probability, their date was earlier than that, almost assuredly dating from A.D. 35-40. The content of the scrolls was identical, even to spacing, to the presently accepted Hebrew Massoretic text.

As quickly as the New Testament books were written and distributed to their various recipients, they began to be copied by devout believers.

But this multiplication of copies in the Greek was insufficient as the gospel soon reached non-Greek speaking peoples. It thus became necessary for the New Testament books to be translated into other languages.

Syriac was the first language into which the New Testament was translated. This was followed by Egyptian, Ethiopian, Armenian, and old Latin translations. The earliest of the translations date to within fifty years of the death of the Apostle John.

The Scriptures were translated into the Germanic, or Gothic, language about A.D. 350. This was the forerunner of the English language. Shortly thereafter Jerome translated the Bible into Latin, and his work became known as the Latin Vulgate. This was for many centuries the official Bible of the Roman Catholic Church. Jerome's was the last translation rendered from the original languages until the Byzantine Empire fell to the Turks in 1454.

Middle History of Translations

In 1378, John Wyclif, with a deep burden that the common man should be able to read the Scriptures in his own language, translated the Latin Vulgate into English. He was rewarded for his efforts by excommunication from the Roman Catholic Church.

The powerful and persuasive influence of the Roman Church resulted in a bill being introduced to the English Parliament to forbid the circulation of English Scriptures. The penalty for possession of a handwritten copy of the banned work was frequently martyrdom. A century elapsed before another English translation of the Bible was rendered.

Exactly one hundred years after the death of Wyclif, William Tyndale was born. Well educated (he knew seven languages) and devout, he spearheaded an effort unsupported by the Church of England to translate the New Testament from the Greek into English.

Hebrew and Greek manuscripts had been unavailable to Wyclif, but they had been brought back to the West by Christians fleeing from the Byzantine Empire at the impending threat of the Turkish invasion. The Eastern church had for many centuries carefully preserved these manuscripts in the original languages while the Western Roman church contented itself with the Latin Scriptures. As a result of the return of the ancient manuscripts and their copies, interest was renewed in the study of Hebrew and Greek.

In 1476 and 1503, respectively, the first Greek and Hebrew grammars were published. The first published Greek New Testament was released by Erasmus in 1516. A Greek scholar, Erasmus had available to him the best of the old Greek manuscripts. It is essentially this text, reflecting the vast majority of Greek manuscripts, that we have today in the Majority Text (also known as the Received Text, the Textus Receptus, the Byzantine Text, or the Traditional Text, with few variations).

When the exiled Tyndale translated the Greek into English, he used the Textus Receptus. Martin Luther did the same when he translated the Scriptures into German.

In the year of 1536, Tyndale was strangled and burned at the stake with a prayer on his lips: "Lord, open the King of England's eyes." His prayer was answered three years later when the Church of England authorized the translation of the Great Bible. This had been preceded, in 1535, by the private printing of the Coverdale Bible. Matthew's Bible (Matthew was a pseudonym for a reformer martyred during the Catholic Queen Mary's reign) appeared in 1537. All of these works, and others, were basically revisions of Tyndale.

When Queen Elizabeth ascended the English throne, the reformers returned to England from Geneva, Switzerland, and brought with them the Genevan Bible. This translation was for sixty years the dominant English Bible. It was the first to be divided into verses and to omit the Apocrypha.

When Elizabeth died in 1603, a distant relative, King James of Scotland, emerged as the heir to the throne. As his entourage wended its way from Scotland to England, he was presented with the Millenary Petition, signed by some 1,000 ministers. Among other things, the petition requested the king to authorize a new translation of the Bible.

Each of the previous translations had its disadvantages: the Great Bible was so called because of its tremendous size, and this made its widespread use impractical; the Genevan Bible, translated under the oversight of John Calvin, included marginal notes offensive to those who held the divine right of kings; Coverdale had made no claim to being the scholar Tyndale was, and his translation was from the German and Latin rather than Hebrew and Greek; the Bishop's Bible was an inferior translation.

In January, 1604, a conference of bishops and Puritan leaders convened at Hampton Court in the presence of King James. Dr. John Reynolds, himself a Puritan, was the spokesman. The king agreed to the request to authorize a new translation, and by the end of July had appointed fifty-four of the greatest scholars in all of England to the task of translating. King James charged that the translation be an exact rendering of the text.

The plan adhered to by the translating committee was detailed and demanding. Each verse of Scripture was gone over fourteen times to gain the maximum expertise of each scholar. Although a vast pool of learning and scholarship was represented by the committee, the translating input was not limited to this. Many learned men were drawn into the project in their particular area of expertise.

The purpose was to give the best rendering of the original languages, and to this end previous translations and commentators were carefully consulted, including Chaldee, Hebrew, Syrian, Greek, Latin, Spanish, French, Italian, and Dutch. The translation was carefully, reverently, cautiously and expertly worked and reworked. The result was that the translation released in 1611 is still considered the masterpiece of the ages, even by its detractors.

Recent History of Translations

In keeping with Christ's command to go and teach all nations, the Holy Spirit has continued to motivate the translating of the Scriptures into the various languages of the world. The same Hebrew and Greek text which was translated in the Authorized Version has now been translated into nearly 900 other languages. God's Word is thus available to men and women everywhere who desire to know Him.

Modern English Translations

While there are today some twenty-five English translations which have received some degree of acceptance, it has been said that there are only two Bibles from which to choose. How can such a simplistic statement be made? The answer is fundamental: there are but two basic texts from which translators work, especially in the New Testament. While they have been identified by various titles, they are simplistically known as the Majority Text and the Minority Text. These two Greek texts differ in no fewer than 6,000 places. They cannot both be completely accurate. The question is, which text is the Word of God?

Majority Text. The Majority Text (Textus Receptus, Received Text, Traditional Text, Byzantine Text) is that from which the King James Bible was rendered. It is the first Greek text published by Erasmus, who worked from manuscripts which represented this textual tradition. There are some 5,225 Greek manuscripts extant today; 80-90% of them are in agreement. This is, of course, why the label "Majority Text" has been given.

The Minority Text. The Minority Text (Wescott-Hort, Nestle, Nestle-Aland, United Bible Societies Greek New Testament) is that from which virtually every English translation since the Revised Version of 1881 has been rendered. While it differs from the Majority Text in some 6,000 places, translations from it into English have an even more pronounced variance. There are some 36,000 differences between the English of the KJV and the RV. This includes entire passages, verses, portions of verses, and single words left out or in some cases added.

While the Majority Text is represented in thousands of Greek manuscripts, the Minority Text is formed essentially by five manuscripts. The most important of the five are Codex Sinaiticus (Aleph) and Codex Vaticanus (B). When these two manuscripts differ, which they do in thousands of places (it is easier to find a verse where they differ than where they agree), preference has traditionally been given to B.

The first edition of this new, minority text was created by the eclecticism of Westcott and Hort, the two chief translators on the committee to produce the Revised Version of 1881. They had collaborated on the text prior to beginning the work of translating, using the recently discovered Aleph and B.

The translating committee was dominated by liberal, even unbelieving churchmen. It included a Unitarian minister who rejected the deity of Christ and rejoiced at the new rendering of I Timothy 3:16. Both Westcott and Hort were sympathetic with Romanism. Another member did not believe the Pentateuch was the work of Moses, and that the Word of God dwelt in many sacred books other than the Bible.

Westcott and Hort had three rules by which they determined, as they compared Greek manuscripts, which reading was most likely to be the original:
- The hardest reading was preferred.
- The reading from which it was most likely that other readings could have developed was to be preferred.
- The shorter reading was to be preferred.

In short, they did not approach their task with a consciousness of the possibility that God had preserved His Word in the vast majority of manuscripts. Rather, they *assumed*, with no proof, that scribes down through the years had simplified and smoothed out readings and conflated (added together) readings from various manuscripts. If, therefore, a reading was smooth and natural, it was suspect. If a manuscript was discovered which had a shorter reading (that is, it left out words) it was thought to be closer to the original.

The faulty text thus created has remained, in its

essential elements, the Greek text from which many translators today work. It is the text seen in the Revised Version, the American Standard Version, the Revised Standard Version, the New American Standard Bible, the New International Version, the New English Bible, Today's English Version, the Amplified Bible, Moffatt's New Translation, and the New Testament in Modern English (Phillips).

The question is very basic: Do we believe God preserved His Word to all generations, as He promised, in the great majority of manuscripts, or do we believe God's Word has been rediscovered within the past century and a half, after having been lost for 1500 years, and that it exists in a mere handful of manuscripts of clumsy workmanship?

Why We Prefer the King James Version

Nearly every new translation takes from the Scriptures. As previously mentioned, the Minority Text differs from the Greek of the Majority Text in some 6,000 places. Some of the more remarkable examples would include John 7:53-8:11; Mark 16:9-20; John 3:13; John 5:4; Acts 8:37; Matthew 17:21; 18:11; 23:14; Mark 11:26; 15:28.

Nearly every new translation makes subtle changes which affect important doctrines. In many cases the Minority Text does not simply delete a word; it changes a word. This results in definite attacks on fundamental doctrines. Some of the striking examples include: Luke 23:42; John 3:16; 6:47; 6:69; 9:35; Romans 1:16; 14:10; Colossians 1:14; I Timothy 3:16.

Some translations are doctrinally biased. The most notable example of this is the *New World Translation,* the official Bible of the Jehovah's Witnesses. While it is supposedly translated from the same eclectic text as the other newer translations, it is further corrupted by strained attempts to make the Scriptures agree with the doctrinal position of its publisher. One glaring example of this bias is John 1:1, "the Word was *a* god." This mistranslation is not attested to by any legitimate translator, including even the most liberal. Were it not for the Watchtower's publication of Benjamin Wilson's *Diaglott*, his work would have fallen into disuse long ago.

Nearly every new translation adds to the Scriptures. Despite the theory that "shorter readings are to be preferred," most new translations adopt longer readings where the Minority Text does so. A notable example of this is I Peter 2:2, where new translations imply that we grow up into salvation.

Some of the new "translations" are in reality paraphrases. A paraphrase is not a translation at all, but a rewording of a translation. The most popular today is *The Living Bible.* In this publication, Kenneth Taylor paraphrased the American Standard Version, the American edition of the Revised Version of 1881. Many of its renderings are merely his comments and opinions without any attempt to be scholarly. This paraphrase should be rejected by Christian people and used only as a commentary, if at all.

Some translations have condensed the Holy Scriptures. The *Reader's Digest Bible* clearly deletes with the editorial pen much of God's Holy Word. While the result no doubt makes interesting reading, it cannot be called the Holy Bible. Jesus said men must live by *every* Word that proceeds from the mouth of God. No human being, regardless of his skill at editing human documents, is qualified to practice on the inspired Scripture.

Some translations have changed meanings. The new "non-sexist" reader published by the National Council of Churches blatantly and with no textual authority eliminates what is considered to be sexist readings in the Holy Scriptures. In a forced effort to eliminate the male image of God presented in the Bible, John 3:16 becomes: "For God so loved the world, that God gave God's only Child, that whoever believes in that Child should not perish but have eternal life." God is no longer the Father but the "Father (and Mother)."

The King James Version is the accepted Bible for use in the United Pentecostal Church.

On May 15, 1953, the Illinois District Conference of the United Pentecostal Church adopted a resolution rejecting the use of the Revised Standard Version in our churches. This resolution was submitted to the General Conference of the United Pentecostal Church International and adopted. A portion of this resolution read: "BE IT FURTHER RESOLVED, that we continue to accept the King James Version of the Bible as the most accurate translation of the Scripture to be used in our churches and among our people."

Although there has been no official statement on the many new translations rendered since the RSV, the same faults which caused us to reject the RSV cause us to reject all the modern speech versions which have followed its example. In addition to the fact that the new translations follow essentially the same Greek text in the New Testament as that followed by the RSV, we can say of the new translations as our brethren did of the RSV: ". . .many of the fundamentals of our Christian faith and doctrine have been changed and are very misleading. . .the majority of the. . .translators. . .are proven to be modernists and liberal scholars. . .and. . .there is no evidence that they hold to the literal complete inspiration of the scriptures."

God continues to honor the King James Bible wherever it is believed and preached. It is the popular standard by which every new translation is compelled to compare itself.

It is possible that a new, accurate updated version could be made from the same text as the King James Version. Indeed, the King James Version was revised in 1629, 1638, 1762, and 1769. In 1982, Thomas Nelson Publishers published its attempt of an updated version with the New King James Version.

We continue to preach the Word with confidence that in the King James Version we actually have the Scriptures. We believe we can hold the Book in our hand and say, "Here is the Word of God!" We are unmoved by the skeptic who points with glee at supposed "contradictions" and discrepancies.

We feel as did the learned Robert Dick Wilson, master of forty-five languages. As he stood before his classes at Princeton Theological Seminary in its conservative days, he would say, "The things I do not understand in the Bible I put down to my own ignorance."

Test Your Knowledge

1. When the sinful king mutilated the original manuscript sent to him by the prophet Jeremiah, no damage was done to the _____ of _____.

2. The Word of God is _____ in Him and is forever settled in _____.

3. _____ was the first language into which the New Testament was translated.

4. _____ first translated the Bible into Latin.

5. John Wyclif, with a burden that the common man should be able to read the Scriptures in his own language, was first to translate the Latin _____ into _____.

6. Wyclif was rewarded for his efforts by _____ from the Roman Catholic Church.

7. William _____, who also pioneered efforts to translate the Scriptures into English, was strangled and burned at the stake.

8. King _____ authorized a new translation of the Scriptures from Greek to English and appointed _____ of the greatest scholars of England to the task.

9. There are basically only two different Greek texts from which translators work: the _____ Text and the _____ Text.

10. The King _____ Bible was translated from the _____ Text.

Apply Your Knowledge

For your own personal information, list the major modern translations of the Bible with which you are familiar. At a library or Christian bookstore, look in the front of each translation you have listed and see the origin and source of the translation. Make special note of the text from which the translations came.

Expand Your Knowledge

If possible you may wish to acquire a copy of the book, *What Was That Verse Again?* by Ben Johnson. You will find this to be an excellent work which will help prepare you for chapter seven. Another book which would be very helpful regarding Bible memorization is *The Memory Book* by Jerry Lucas and Harry Lorraine.

Read the verses of Scripture under "Start With the Scriptures" before beginning chapter seven.

7 Hiding the Word

"Thy word have I hid in mine heart, that I might not sin against thee."

Psalm 119:11

Start with the Scriptures

Joshua 1:8   Psalm 1

Our sympathies are aroused when we hear of Christians in lands where it is unlawful to own a Bible. We should indeed pray for them and do anything within our power to see that copies of the Scriptures are made available to them.

But most Christians regardless of government stance on this issue, have the Bible to read and study. The verses of Scripture a person commits to memory, however, are the only ones he has when he lays his head down in the darkness of the night, when he is working on the job or driving the highway, and when he is faced with a crisis situation which demands an immediate response from the Word of God.

Because of the scarcity of printed Bibles, many Christians in oppressed lands commit vast portions of the Scriptures to memory. Thus it is possible that they sometimes have a better grasp of the Scriptures than those who take the printed Bible for granted.

While Christians should treasure their printed Bibles and be ever grateful to the Lord for making them available, we should also recognize the importance of the many biblical commands to go beyond reading to memorization. This can be done by any Christian, whether or not he has previously been successful in attempts to memorize. Bible memorization should be viewed as necessary, not optional.

David said, "Thy word have I hid in mine heart, that I might not sin against thee" (Psalm 119:11).

One way to hide the Word of God in one's heart is through memorization. As David indicated, this is one of the most powerful deterrents against temptation. Jesus Himself, when faced with Satan's temptations following His fast, resisted by quoting aloud from the Scriptures.

The Rewards of Knowing the Word

Joshua was chosen by the Lord to assume the leadership role vacated by Moses' death. In His preliminary instructions to Joshua, the Lord included a commandment which would insure Joshua's success: "This book of the law shall not depart out of thy mouth; but thou shalt meditate therein day and night, that thou mayest observe to do according to all that is written therein: for then thou shalt make thy way prosperous, and then thou shalt have good success" (Joshua 1:8).

The first part of the commandment had to do with speaking or quoting the Word of God. Never was Joshua to depart from the practice of speaking the Word. He was to forsake his own words in favor of God's Word. When faced with a decision, he was not to rely on human wisdom, but on "thus saith the Lord." This apparently required memorization, for there was no pocket-sized Testament that Joshua could carry about with him to flip through when in need.

The second part of the commandment had to do with meditation. In its strictest sense, meditation is simply *thinking*. Every human being is a master at meditation.

Meditation is not necessarily a sophisticated art which requires great training; it is simply *thinking* Scripture. Meditation does, however, require memorization. Joshua was to meditate in the Word of God day and night. This supersedes carrying a copy of Scripture from which to read; it speaks of Bible memorization.

The third part of the commandment had to do with obedience. As much as a Christian may want to obey God, he will never be successful until he has first committed himself to memorizing, meditating, and speaking the Word of God. Actions are the products of thoughts. Wrong thoughts produce wrong actions; right thoughts produce right actions. The significance of this is seen in Romans 12:2.

The final part of Joshua 1:8 reveals the results of memorization, meditation, and speaking the Word of God. "Thou shalt make thy way prosperous, and then thou shalt have good success." What, or who, determines the level of success and prosperity in an individual's life? *"Thou shalt make thy way prosperous."* When an individual is obedient to the command God gave Joshua, he sets in motion a chain of events which will invariably result in biblical prosperity and success.

It is important that the Scriptures be memorized *exactly;* we are not to add to or take away from the Word of God. This produces great confidence and comfort.

A casual attitude toward the Word of God has produced many pseudo-scriptures. But the Word of God is of such vast importance that one cannot afford to have any less than the highest regard for it.

Devotional Reading of the Word

Although Timothy's father was a Greek and evidently an unbeliever, Timothy grew up with strong faith. This was largely imparted to him by his godly grandmother and mother. (See II Timothy 1:5.) What means did these women use to impart faith to young Timothy? They faithfully taught him the Scriptures. "And that from a child thou hast known the holy scriptures, which are able to make thee wise unto salvation through faith which is in Christ Jesus" (II Timothy 3:15).

For the Word of God to have its full impact on an individual, he must be exposed to it daily; he cannot limit his interest in the Word to public church meetings. The Word of God should be read privately and as a family. A pivotal commandment of the Old Testament, Deuteronomy 6:4-15, contains this statement: "And these words, which I command thee this day, shall be in thine heart: And thou shalt teach them diligently unto thy children, and shalt talk of them when thou sittest in thine house, and when thou walkest by the way, and when thou liest down, and when thou risest up" (Deuteronomy 6:6-7).

Each person should have a personal, daily time of communication with the Lord. For different people this will take various forms, but it should include

Bible reading and prayer.

Christians should not hesitate to mark their Bibles when a truth is made clear to them. Use of a notebook to record insights gained during devotional time is a simple method of making the time more meaningful and productive.

Family devotions are also of great value in establishing the atmosphere of a Christ-centered home. Such a practice also provides a regular opportunity to teach both by example and word. As with personal devotions, family devotions will take many forms.

Many families have been frustrated in their attempts to establish a pattern of devotions and have given up. A simple guideline is to allow this to be a relaxed, informal time. It should be enjoyable and even fun for younger children. Parents may wish to introduce handcrafts, read Christian stories, look at selected pictures, or listen to story records or tapes. It is possible for as much creativity to go into this as into a well-prepared Sunday school class.

The Bible example, rather than giving a rigid, formal time of instruction, says the teaching is to be accomplished throughout the normal process of the day: rising, walking, sitting, lying down. Parents should realize that the most powerful way to indoctrinate their children in God's truth is to interweave it into all the affairs of life. This does not mean that the parent will quote a verse of Scripture in response to every question the child asks, but that the parent's response will always reflect the truth of God's Word.

Public Reading of the Word

At the end of every seven years in the nation of Israel the law was to be read publicly in the hearing of all the people. This included not only the men, but also the women, children, and strangers. The purpose was that the Israelites would hear and learn the Scriptures, fear God, and observe His commandments. This regular public reading also served an important function in the preservation of the Scriptures. (See Deuteronomy 31:9-13.)

Upon the return of Israel from Babylonian captivity, Ezra read publicly from the law in the hearing of all the people. They were attentive and responded with worship and praise as the Word was read distinctly. Rejoicing swept through the congregation, and the people ate, drank, and sent gifts to others. In the words of the Scriptures, they made "great mirth, because they had understood the words that were declared unto them." (See Nehemiah 8:1-12.)

There is a definite place for public reading of the Word of God in today's church. Sometimes it is read by the minister alone from the pulpit, sometimes a responsive reading is used, and sometimes the congregation joins the minister in reading an entire passage aloud. Whatever the format, the Word should always be read or heard with great attentiveness, and the response should be joy that the Word of God is available to us and that it can be understood.

The significance of God's Word is never to be minimized. According to the Scriptures, God has magnified His Word above all His name. (See Psalm 138:2.)

Benefits of Memorizing the Word

At many points the Scriptures assume that a faithful man is memorizing the Word of God. One example among many is Psalm 1. "Blessed is the man that walketh not in the counsel of the ungodly, nor standeth in the way of sinners, nor sitteth in the seat of the scornful. But his delight is in the law of the LORD; and in his law doth he meditate day and night" (Psalm 1:1-2).

The latter phrase, "in his law doth he meditate day and night," assumes memorization. Other such examples are David's statement in Psalm 119:11 and the commandment of the Lord to Joshua in Joshua 1:8.

Few Christians would question the importance of memorizing Scriptures, but many are convinced that they are unable to memorize or that the task would be so difficult as to outweigh the rewards. This is a false assumption. All people *do* memorize. And whatever effort may be involved in memorizing Scriptures, the rewards far outweigh the sacrifice.

Many books are available on memory techniques. Indeed, many things can be done to improve one's ability to memorize. Ben E. Johnson, in his book *What Was That Verse Again?* (Santa Barbara, CA: Quill Publications, 1976) suggests seven principles to aid memorization.

Memorize the general thought. Before attempting to memorize a portion of Scripture word-for-word, review it sufficiently to grasp the general content. A clear understanding of the relationship of concepts and themes will make detailed memorizing easier.

Intend to remember. Many things are forgotten simply because there is no commitment to memorization. An intention to memorize will increase one's alertness.

React actively. There are two types of memory—passive and active. Passive memory is automatic. Some events are of such magnitude that they impress themselves on memory and are recalled with little or no effort. Active memory requires effort. The remaining four principles are ways in which active memory is acquired.

Repeat it. Repetition, or rote memory, has always been effective in memorizing. However, the manner and frequency of repetition can greatly affect the effectiveness of memorization. Johnson points out, "In one study which compared the results of rereading technical material five times in one day with reading it once a day for five days, a month after reading, those who had reread it five times spread out over five days could recall nearly three times as much as the others who had reread it five times in one day."

Write It Down—Say It Aloud. To write out in longhand the Scriptures being memorized will greatly aid in retention.

Saying the Scriptures repeatedly aloud is also an effective way to impress them on the memory. The auditory track of the mind is thus reinforcing the visual track. Memorization will increase with the impact made upon the senses maximized.

Group things together. If things are broken down into smaller units, they will be easier to grasp. It may, for instance, be easier to memorize several verses from various passages which deal with the same subject than to memorize the same number of verses from a single passage in which the subject changes.

Review regularly. Johnson remarks, "Most adults will forget two-thirds of everything they read within 24 hours and about 90% within a week. Forgetting...is enormous...the first few days, almost as bad...the first two weeks, but slows down after that. Therefore anything you can retain for the first two weeks has every chance of staying with you permanently." Regular review during the first two weeks that the material is memorized will greatly enhance permanent memory.

Meditating On the Word

The Institute in Basic Youth Conflicts has suggested three steps involved in meditation. They are:

- *Memorize.* It is obviously impossible to meditate on that which has not first been memorized.
- *Personalize.* When a passage has been thoroughly memorized, insert the first person into it and quote it aloud back to God. For example, Psalm 1:2 would personalize something like this: "My delight will be in the law of the LORD, and in His law will I meditate day and night."
- *Visualize.* This involves picturing each word. As it applies to Psalm 1:1, the question would be asked, "What does *blessed* mean?" Does this word provoke any visual ideas? Specific blessings? What about the word *man?*

The individual meditating can put himself in that place. The word *walketh* is easily visualized, as is *sitteth* and *standeth*. As each word is visualized, new and rich insights into the passage will come to mind.

The Word of God is the very basis of the Christian life. Nothing can substitute for a knowledge of the Word, reading the Word, memorizing the Word, and meditating on the Word. A faithful commitment to these practices will give a Christian new power, direction, and purpose. In short, he will begin to fulfill the biblical injunction to not live by bread alone, but "by every word that proceedeth out of the mouth of God" (Matthew 4:4).

Test Your Knowledge

Hidden in the following puzzle are key words of this chapter which are listed below. Find each one, circle it and consider its relation to this lesson.

Scriptures	Heart	Communication
Memorize	Temptations	Preservation
Committed	Success	Repetition
Possess	Meditate	Write
Appreciation	Daily	Visualize

```
F A N Y G Y A C M S H P D A X F D C
M G J E U G S E E F R B R U X N Q Y
N F A T N G D R A E E Q Z R Y N A U
D K S N Z I U X S H Z H A T V T R W
P L T Z T T P E S U C C E S S E T C
F I Z A P O R N K J M N Y A O M W P
N E T I S V N O I T A I C E R P P A
G E R S A X V I Z C T L W L O T Y U
P C E T W D N T U D K J Y Y R A H P
S S I L Q E M A B Y A A J X E T M Y
S O J G I T Z C V Z G I N J P I E A
N E E I S T Z I X M U G L L E O M B
O Z P F N I Q N L M I T F Y T N O P
E I T G X M O U I A Y X U N I S R W
O T G A K M X M N T U G T S T K I B
E N I A X O X M N Y D S O K I V Z V
C X K R K C O O L Y R B I X O X E H
H W F R W I U C G T O X M V N P W P
```

Apply Your Knowledge

It would be an excellent challenge to your class to memorize a portion of Scripture together. The discipline of doing this within the framework of a class could help students begin a lifelong pursuit of Bible memorization.

A portion of Scripture which would be appropriate for such a beginning is Psalm 1. If your class would set a goal of memorizing one verse from this Psalm each day, the entire Psalm would be memorized by your next class session. Individuals could then quote the Psalm publicly, or the class could quote it as a group.

Expand Your Knowledge

The next chapter is about studying the Word of God. In preparation for the study read the verses of Scripture listed under "Start With the Scriptures." Also, gather together any and all of the various Bible study aids you may have for reference while studying the chapter.

8 Studying the Word

> "Study to shew thyself approved unto God, a workman that needeth not to be ashamed, rightly dividing the word of truth."
>
> II Timothy 2:15

Start with the Scriptures

John 5:39
Acts 17:11
II Timothy 4:13

The Importance of Studying the Word

We live in a time of famine for the Word of God (Amos 8:11-12). Many people do not desire sound doctrine, but follow false teachers who tickle their ears by proclaiming only what they want to hear (II Timothy 4:3-4). However, we will find the message of salvation only through the Word of God.

Jesus told the Pharisees, "Search the scriptures; for in them ye think ye have eternal life: and they are they which testify of me" (John 5:39). The Jews correctly believed that the Scriptures revealed the way of salvation. Jesus did not rebuke them for this; rather, He commanded them to study the Scriptures. As the context of this passage makes clear, He rebuked them for rejecting Him—the One to whom the Scriptures pointed.

The Jews in Berea are an interesting contrast to this. Paul and Silas came to Berea after unbelieving Jews in Thessalonica forced them to leave that city. When they preached the gospel of Jesus the Messiah, the Berean Jews studied the Scriptures to see if this doctrine were true. The Bible calls them "more noble than those in Thessalonica, in that they received the word with all readiness of mind, and searched the scriptures daily, whether those things were so" (Acts 17:11). As a result many of them believed and received salvation (Acts 17:12).

Some people think that the less they study the Bible, the less God will require of them. However, ignorance is no excuse. In these latter days, God has revealed His message of repentance to all the world. "And the times of this ignorance God winked at; but now commandeth all men every where to repent" (Acts 17:30). In particular, willful ignorance is not an excuse but an indictment.

We are admonished to study or be diligent to receive the approval of God, thereby avoiding shame. (See II Timothy 2:15.) We do this by "rightly dividing" or correctly handling the word of truth, treating it in a workmanlike fashion. In other words, if we expect to receive God's approval we must diligently read, study, interpret, preach, and teach the Bible in a careful, thorough, and correct manner.

In short, the Bible is our sole authority for doctrine and instruction in salvation (II Timothy 3:15-17). We must judge preachers, angels, utterances, and spirits by the Word. (See Deuteronomy 13:1-4; Galatians 1:8-9; I Corinthians 14:29, 37; I John 4:1.) Only by studying God's Word do we have protection against false prophets, false doctrines, and satanic spirits.

How to Study the Word

A good way to study the Bible is to study it book by book while reading it daily. For each book, the reader should obtain information about the author, original audience, date and place of writing, and purpose of the book. There are several suggestions which may help a person study God's Word.
- Outline the book, chapter or passage
- Define key words
- Research cross references
- Make marginal notations
- Underline, highlight, or color key words and phrases

In addition to studying the Bible book by book, there are other valuable approaches. Often, the Bible student will want to pick a certain subject—such as atonement, holiness, water baptism, or angels—and research it throughout the Bible. It is helpful to color-code key doctrinal topics: for example, water baptism—green; Holy Spirit baptism—yellow; oneness—red; holiness—blue. Also, a biographical study of a certain character such as David or Paul can be very rewarding.

For Bible study to be profitable, it should be much more than a dry academic exercise; it should be part of a total devotional life that includes faithful prayer and church attendance.

Tools for Study

Some people take pride in using no other books in their study of the Bible. While each person does have the capacity to read, understand, and obey the message of Scripture, the product of centuries of linguistic, archeological, and cultural research can certainly aid our understanding of the Bible. Paul apparently used reference materials in studying the Scriptures, for he asked Timothy to bring to him his books and parchments (II Timothy 4:13).

There are numerous tools for biblical study available today.

Study Bibles. Most Bibles have scripture references in the margin which direct the reader to other passages on the same subject. Many Bibles have a number of aids such as marginal notes, chain references, concordances, maps, outlines, and other various helps.

Concordances. A concordance lists the various places in Scripture where a certain word occurs. It is useful in locating certain verses and in studying particular subjects. An exhaustive concordance, such as *Strong's Exhaustive Concordance,* lists every occurrence of every word in Scripture.

Word study aids. There are a number of expository dictionaries or word studies available, such as those by Vine, Nelson, Wilson, Robertson, Vincent, and Wuest. Rather than giving definitions of English words, these books give definitions of the underlying Hebrew and Greek words, providing invaluable help to those who do not know the original languages of the Scriptures.

For those who know the Hebrew and Greek alphabets, lexicons are very useful. A lexicon is a dictionary with word entries in the original language and definitions in English. Lexicons coded to *Strong's Exhaustive Concordance* are available for those who know only English.

Bible dictionaries and encyclopedias. This type of reference gives extensive information on Bible subjects such as people, places, animals, plants, and culture.

Atlases. An atlas is useful in studying such things as journeys, wars, lives of Bible characters, and prophecy.

Commentaries. A commentary discusses and explains the biblical text. It brings together knowledge gleaned from various sources (such as the ones mentioned above) in order to unfold the full meaning of the passage under discussion. Commentaries are very helpful in presenting detailed analyses, new avenues of thought, alternative interpretations, and explanations of difficult passages. Naturally, information gleaned from various commentaries should be carefully evaluated in the light of all biblical truth and thought.

Translations. Various translations present different shades of meaning and alternative word choices suggested by the original language text. They can serve as an abbreviated form of word study or commentary. New revisions, such as the *New King James Version,* modernize words that are obscure and archaic. Care should be exercised in the use of translations, however, as pointed out in chapter six. Not all translations have come from reliable texts.

Ten Principles of Biblical Interpretation

In order to understand the Bible as we study it, we must interpret it correctly. The art and science of biblical interpretation is called hermeneutics. The following points are ten important principles of hermeneutics.

We should use the literal method of interpreting the Scriptures rather than the allegorical method. This means to follow the natural or usual implication of an expression—the ordinary and apparent meaning of the words. By contrast, the allegorical method seeks to find a hidden, "spiritual" meaning beneath the apparent one.

The illumination of the Spirit is necessary. The carnal mind cannot understand the things of God (Romans 8:7; I Corinthians 2:11-16). We should study the Word of God prayerfully, letting God's Spirit enlighten our minds and lead us into truth (John 15:26; 16:12-13; I John 2:20-27). A Christian should not divorce Bible study from his total spiritual experience and relationship with the living Christ.

The Scriptures are basically plain and meant to be understood. No essential doctrine is hidden in obscure passages. Difficulties in understanding the Scriptures usually arise because of a person's cultural, linguistic, and contextual distance from the original text or because of his lack of spiritual illumination.

The Bible is accommodated to the human mind. The Bible has to express truth in finite human vocabulary and thought patterns, although it never accommodates to error. Sometimes, biblical language does not teach a physical or earthly literalism, but presents greater spiritual truth in ways that man can understand best. For example, the Bible describes God as having a heart, eyes, ears, nostrils, and wings, but He is not a giant human, beast, or fowl. The gold on heaven's streets is not earthly gold; it is transparent. Hellfire is not an earthly fire; it is eternal and in a place of outer darkness.

God reveals truth progressively from Old Testament to New Testament. There is a progression from material to spiritual, as spiritual truths are first taught in physical types.

Scriptures interpret Scriptures. The whole Bible is the context for interpreting a passage. Clear verses help interpret obscure ones.

The Scriptures are unified. They teach one

theology with no internal contradictions. We should seek to harmonize all passages.

No doctrine stands totally on one passage alone. God uses two or three witnesses to establish truth (II Corinthians 13:1). We should not ignore or discount any passage, but if someone bases a certain doctrine solely on one passage, he is probably misinterpreting it.

Each passage has one primary meaning, but can have many applications. We should first seek the meaning before making applications.

We should use sound rules of logic; God is not illogical.

Using the Literal Method

The first principle listed above, using the literal method, is so crucial that we should consider it further. Following are ten aspects of finding the literal meaning of a text.

The literal method consists of exegesis (bringing meaning out of the text) not eisogesis (putting meaning into the text). We approach a passage by asking, "What does the text say?" not "How does it support my view?" or "What do I want it to say?"

Word study. We seek the basic, customary, socially designated meaning of the words as defined in the original language and culture.

Grammar. Sentence structure, punctuation, parentheticals, gender (masculine, feminine, neuter), tense (past, present, future, etc.), case (subjective, objective, etc.), number (singular, plural), and pronoun antecedents all affect the meaning of a passage.

Background. To understand a passage fully, we should find out information on the author or speaker (who), the original audience (to whom), the occasion (when, where, how) and the purpose (why). Is the speaker approved of God or not? Does the Bible merely record what he said and did or does it also endorse what he said and did? Would our interpretation have been comprehensible to the original audience? Is our interpretation consistent with the original occasion and purpose?

Context. We should consider the sentence, passage, book, testament, and entire Bible. How does the whole sentence or passage shed light on a particular word or phrase? How does a certain passage fit in with the theme of the whole book? Does it make a difference that this passage is in the Gospels rather than in Acts, or in the Old Testament rather than in the New Testament? How do parallel passages and cross references aid our understanding?

Figures of speech and symbols. The literal method does not exclude these, but recognizes them whenever the immediate context clearly indicates them. The Bible uses them much as we do in communication today—not to be taken in a grossly literal way but to express truth in a poetic or figurative fashion. Examples are metaphor (Hebrews 12:29), simile (Exodus 24:17), hyperbole (Judges 7:12), personification (Proverbs 1:20-33), metonymy (Psalm 51:18), synedoche (Genesis 3:19; Mark 1:5), and irony (I Kings 18:27; 22:15).

Literary genre (style). The Bible contains many distinct literary styles, such as history, poetry, wisdom literature, apocalyptic, preaching, and teaching. The identification of these styles will affect the way we approach certain passages. For example, a phrase in Revelation is more likely to be symbolic than if it were found in Acts.

Biblical history, geography, and culture. Many names, objects, places, and events are obscure without some knowledge in these areas.

Interpretation of parables. A parable is a true-to-life story told to illustrate one central truth. In general, the details do not have independent significance but are simply inserted to make the story realistic. It is a mistake to attach doctrinal meaning to every detail unless the Bible does so.

Interpretation of types. A type is something in the Old Testament that had a real existence of its own but which foreshadowed or prefigured a permanent and greater truth in the New Testament. The student cannot invent types; a type originates in the intention and purpose of God. A valid type is either designed in the New Testament or can be inferred from New Testament material on typology.

An Example—Matthew 28:19

These principles of biblical interpretation can be illustrated by studying the question of baptismal formula raised by Matthew 28:19. In that verse, Jesus commanded His disciples to baptize "in the name of the Father, and of the Son, and of the Holy Ghost." We later find those disciples baptizing "in the name of Jesus Christ" (Acts 2:38; 8:16; 10:48; 19:5; 22:16). How are we to interpret the words of Matthew 28:19?

Applying the principles of hermeneutics, we should interpret the verse literally, asking God to illuminate the meaning by His Spirit and believing that He meant for us to understand the meaning. Moreover, the Scriptures interpret Scriptures, so the Book of Acts shows how the apostles interpreted and obeyed this verse. Other passages show that Jesus Christ is the Father, Son, and Holy Ghost (Isaiah 9:6; II Corinthians 3:17; Colossians 2:9) and that the name of Father, Son, and Holy Ghost is Jesus (Matthew 1:21; John 5:43; 14:26).

Since the Scriptures are unified we seek an explanation that will harmonize Matthew and Acts. We reject any argument that concedes a contradiction, such as, "I would rather accept the words of Jesus than the words of Peter."

No doctrine rests solely on one passage, so we cannot build our theology on Matthew 28:19 alone without considering other passages. In fact, since so many passages speak of baptism in the name of Jesus, Matthew 28:19 is apparently the more indirect passage that should be interpreted in light of the others rather than vice versa.

Finally, we can apply the rules of logic and prayerfully reason through to a logical explanation.

In applying the literal method, several factors are very significant. Word studies will show us the true meaning of *baptize, name, Father, Son, Holy Ghost*. For example, the Holy Ghost is literally the one holy Spirit; that is, God Himself. An analysis of the grammar reveals that *name* is singular, denoting the one supreme name of the One Being who is at once Father, Son, and Spirit.

Looking at the background, Jesus was speaking to His close disciples who were strictly monotheistic Jews. He was not trying to reveal to them a radically new concept of the Godhead nor did they receive it as such. He knew they would understand the terminology He used.

Looking to context, Jesus said He had all power (verse 18), *therefore* baptize converts in the name (verse 19) and teach them His commandments (verse 20). Since Jesus was speaking of *His* power, *His* followers, and *His* commandments, He was evidently speaking of *His* name. Parallel passages of this same commission also describe the name of Jesus (Mark 16:17; Luke 24:47). The total context thus indicates that the name Matthew 28:19 describes is Jesus.

This example illustrates the importance of studying the Bible.

Test Your Knowledge

Match the following references to their descriptions.

A. Study Bible
B. Concordance
C. Word Study Aids
D. Bible Dictionary
E. Atlas
F. Commentary
G. Translations

_____ 1. Expository dictionaries, lexicons, interlinears and other reference works which refer to the original language.

_____ 2. Various versions of the Bible which give alternate word choices and varying shades of meaning.

_____ 3. This book discusses and explains the biblical text.

_____ 4. Bible which includes margin references, maps, concordance, outlines, and other helps.

_____ 5. A book of maps of Bible times.

_____ 6. A study book which gives extensive information on Bible subjects.

_____ 7. Book that lists all the places in the Bible where a certain word appears.

Apply Your Knowledge

Take the Epistle of Paul to Titus, or the Bible Book of your choice, and begin a Bible study of the Book. Titus would be a good Book with which to begin as it is short and yet offers a beautiful and interesting text for study.

Expand Your Knowledge

Before proceeding to chapter nine, define the following words using a good dictionary. Write each word on a sheet of paper and then define each one: divide; declare; preach; teach; expound; debate; doctrine; dogma.

Rightly Dividing the Word 9

"For I have not shunned to declare unto you all the counsel of God."

Acts 20:27

Start with the Scriptures

Romans 10:13-18
I Corinthians 1:17-25
II Timothy 3:15; 4:2

Paul wrote to Timothy that one result of studying the Word of God was the skill of "rightly dividing the word of truth" (II Timothy 2:15). Some people today think that "rightly dividing" implies that parts of the Bible are no longer relevant to modern Christianity. They assume it takes much study to be able to weed out (divide) those irrelevant portions of Scripture. We will discover in this chapter what "rightly dividing" really means.

Declaring the Word

Paul wrote that he had not refrained from declaring all the counsel of God (Acts 20:27). Paul felt it was important that the Word of God be declared. It is still important that it be declared.

A variety of words were used in the Bible to show how the Word was to be declared:

- *Preach.* The Early Church, scattered due to persecution, "went every where preaching the word" (Acts 8:4).
- *Teach.* The converted Paul "taught. . .publickly, and from house to house" (Acts 20:20).
- *Expound.* The husband and wife team of Aquila and Priscilla took into their fellowship an eloquent preacher named Apollos who was known to be knowledgeable in the Scriptures, and they "Expounded unto him the way of God more perfectly" (Acts 18:26).
- *Debate.* Paul "disputed" with the religious men of his day over their doctrines (Acts 19:8-9).

In whatever form, whether in speech or in print, whether giving instructions for godly living or disputing false doctrines, it is imperative that the Word of God be declared to all men.

The Delight of Declaring the Word

There is a joy that comes in declaring the Word of God. Even persecution cannot destroy it (Acts 13:49-52). Paul wrote a letter declaring the way of the Lord to the Corinthian church that made them "sorry," and he admitted that he did "repent," apparently for the letter's tone. But when that letter proved to bring repentance, a change of ways to the Corinthians, then Paul wrote, "Now I rejoice, not that ye were made sorry, but that ye sorrowed to repentance" (II Corinthians 7:9).

In the same sense, an evangelist feels great joy when at the end of his sermon sinners come to repentance. Likewise, pastors feel great joy as they see their sermons and Bible studies working changes in the lives of church members. Sunday school teachers know great joy when a student under their direction begins to show spiritual maturity. Youth workers rejoice when they see rebellion transformed into submission due to their efforts in declaring the Word of the Lord. A parent knows intense joy when his children seek to know the God he or she has declared to them. Any Christian who sits down on a couch with a friend and declares the Word of the Lord to him will feel overwhelming joy when that friend gives his life to Jesus Christ as a result of such declaration.

One lady who had been filled with the Holy Spirit for many years went to her pastor and exclaimed, "I just don't feel happy anymore!" Once it was determined that there was no evident reason for her unhappiness, the wise pastor investigated her spiritual habits and discovered she had never won a soul to the Lord. He encouraged her to focus all her energy on one soul and determine that she would win that soul within a year.

She did, and within the time period won a friend to God. The result was a happiness she had never known! She became an active soulwinner, a true declarer of the Word, and never reverted to her former state of unhappiness.

The Destination of Declaring the Word

The ultimate aim or destination of a Christian who sets out to declare the counsel of God is not, however, a personal feeling of joy. It is to effect a change in the destiny of the hearer. Of temporal importance, one hopes to effect a change in the daily habits or behavior of the hearer, but ultimately one who declares the Word of God is hoping to save a soul from hell.

Two scriptural mandates are worthy of scrutiny. The first is Christ's instruction concerning Himself as the object of salvation. Jesus likens Himself to the "door," and anyone who "entereth not by the door into the sheepfold, but climbeth up some other way, the same is a thief and a robber." (See John 10:1-10.) The second is that "it pleased God by the foolishness of preaching to save them that believe" (I Corinthians 1:21). A close look at each follows.

A Deity Worth Declaring

There is a frightening trend in many churches to reduce Jesus to *a* christ, not *the* Christ. A renowned minister was once interviewed on a nationwide broadcast. He was asked by a member of the audience if he thought that everyone had to be saved in the same manner he had been. His reply became an attack on the deity of Jesus Christ.

He stated that no one had to be saved like he had been, and proceeded to offer his description of Christ's role in salvation. He described Jesus as a "great light," of which there are many "broken lights," or "lesser lights." If someone could not comprehend the brilliance of that "bright light," but could focus on one of the many "lesser lights," then so be it! He felt that as long as the lesser lights were pointing the way to God, then it would matter little to God if a man had not been able to accept Jesus Christ as the only "light."

Let it be forever settled, however, that Jesus Christ is not one of many; He is the only begotten Son of God, the only image of the one true God. (See John 3:16; Hebrews 1:3.)

Jesus said of Himself, "I am the way, the truth,

and the life: no man cometh unto the Father, but by me" (John 14:6). Of all the doctrines His Word gives us to declare unto the world, perhaps nothing is more significant than declaring who He is—the Lord Jesus Christ. The question He asked His disciples is still asked of men today. "But whom do ye say that I am?" And the answer today must be the same as the one Peter gave. "Thou art the Christ, the Son of the living God." (See Matthew 16:15-16.)

A Design for Declaring the Word

If a Christian decides he is going to be a declarer of the Word but starts off without a plan, possessing only a determination to succeed, he might do well. He could also fail, however, because good intentions without a plan, aim or goal, usually end in frustration. A few instructions and assurances might help to organize a planned approach for declaring the Word of God.

Who can declare the Word of God? You can, and you should. God is counting on you to "declare" Him to the world. It is a true saying that if God has any hands, they are your hands; if God has any feet, they are your feet; and if He has a mouth, it is your mouth. Modern schools will not declare His Word nor will government agencies. Church services may declare Him, but only to those who attend them. If His Word is declared to the world, it will be by people like you.

Where can a person declare His Word? Any Christian can declare His Word wherever he goes. As Saul began to go from house to house persecuting Christians, his efforts succeeded in scattering them. Yet even as Christians were being scattered, they "went every where preaching the word" (Acts 8:4). Any place is a good place to tell the unsaved about God.

In Acts 8 we read of Philip's going to Samaria and having a great revival. He may have had no pulpit, but he knew how to declare the Word of the Lord. The Samaritans were blessed because he did.

To whom can a Christian declare it? To everyone! Paul said he was a "debtor both to the Greeks, and to the Barbarians; both to the wise, and to the unwise" (Romans 1:14). All people need to hear the gospel, and Christians are obligated to go beyond boundaries of race or status and preach the Word of God to every person.

Declare it with confidence. Paul was able, though he was a prisoner, to declare the Word of God with confidence (Acts 28:31). As a person talks to others about their souls, he should be confident that God is pleased with his efforts, and that results will come. God will confirm His Word. "And they went forth, and preached every where, the Lord working with them, and confirming the word with signs following" (Mark 16:20).

Declare it with boldness. After being confronted by the chief priests and elders for declaring Jesus, Peter and John and the rest of their company began to pray. They asked God to give them boldness, and they asked Him to give it by performing signs and wonders (Acts 4:29-30). "And when they had prayed. . .they were all filled with the Holy Ghost, and they spake the word of God with boldness" (Acts 4:31).

They asked for signs and miracles. It is not hard for a Christian to be bold when it is obvious that the power of God is working in his behalf. It appears, however, that the Lord responded to their praying by filling them full of His Spirit, and *that* "filling" enabled them to speak with boldness.

Boldness to speak the Word of God is not acquired by developing a positive self-image only, but by being filled with the Holy Ghost, an experience which comes only by obedience to the Word and promise of God.

Declare it with power. Paul apparently did not spend much time practicing his speaking manners. Apparently he did not invest his time in coining new and "catchy" phrases. Instead, he said, "My speech and my preaching was not with enticing words of man's wisdom, but in demonstration of the Spirit and of power: That your faith should not stand in the wisdom of men, but in the power of God" (I Corinthians 2:4-5).

We should not be concerned with making a good impression through our choice of words. Our concern should be that the power of God accompanies our words.

Dividing or Declaring the Word?

This chapter thus far has offered instructions for declaring the Word of God. The title of the chapter, however, is "Rightly Dividing the Word." The word *dividing* comes from the Greek word *orthotomeo* which translates "to dissect (expound) correctly (the divine message)."

Some people mistakenly believe that parts of the Bible are no longer relevant. Believing some portions of Scripture to be outdated, they spend much time trying to sort out which is applicable today and which is not. For example, one group completely eliminates the Old Testament as being "not for us today." Another group does away with key passages in the New Testament concerning the gifts of the Spirit by claiming those gifts are "not for the church today." Yet another group seeks to label Paul a male chauvinist and declare all his teachings concerning women "not for the church today." But every true Christian must believe that "All scripture is given by inspiration of God, and is profitable for doctrine, for reproof, for correction, for instruction in righteousness" (II Timothy 3:16).

Paul encouraged Timothy to study so that he might be able to "rightly divide" the Word of God. Since *dividing* (*orthotomeo*) means "expounding," why did Paul not use a word that simply meant "expounding"? He could have used another word and been clear in that meaning, but something unique is added to the verse by use of the word *dividing*.

Adam Clarke offers this in his commentary: "Therefore, by 'rightly dividing the word of truth,' we are able to understand his continuing in the true doctrine, and teaching that to every person; and according to our Lord's simile, giving each his portion of meat in due season—milk to babes, strong meat to the full grown, comfort to the disconsolate, reproof to the irregular and careless; in a word, finding out the necessities of his hearer, and preaching so as to meet those necessities."

A wise "workman" will know which portions of Scripture to distribute to others as he deals with them in their situations. The Bible admonishes us to be prepared to give a "reason of the hope" that is in us (I Peter 3:15).

To the depressed, there is a verse that will offer cheer. To the angry, there is a verse that will calm the storm. To the ignorant, there is a verse that will enlighten. To the rebellious, there is a word that will rebuke. To the sorrowful, there is a word of comfort. The wise Christian should so study to become a veritable encyclopedia of Bible knowledge, able to supply to every man the portion of Scripture needed.

Declaring All the Word

First, a person must study "all" the Word, and then he can, as Paul did, declare "all the counsel of God" (Acts 20:27).

The pitfall of becoming "theme-oriented" should be avoided. Without proper study a person may become fluent in discussing one point of doctrine while remaining ignorant in others. When that is the case, the one who is witnessing is always trying to steer the conversation toward areas in which he can converse. If the person being witnessed to asks many questions which cannot be answered, he will soon lose interest in the discussion. It is urgent, therefore, that a true Christian study "all" the Word of God.

C. H. Spurgeon recommended in *Lectures To My Students:* "A fellow should get all the knowledge he can, but in his getting not forget to get the most important knowledge—the knowledge of the Word of God. Study history, law, and any other subject of interest," he suggested, "but do not forget that the Bible is the most important book of all." Not just some of the Bible, but all of it.

There is a story about a man who was being led to the gallows in England many years ago. He was a criminal who no doubt deserved his punishment. The law required that a priest accompany him to the gallows. The priest followed behind in the procession, reading and chanting select verses from the Bible, some of which pertained to hell. Upon reaching the gallows, the prisoner was given a chance to speak his last words, which went something like this: "If I really believed all that stuff you say you believe, if I really believed there was a hell, I'd crawl across England on my knees to warn men of that place."

Shallow knowledge in some areas of the Bible may imply to the sinner that we really do not believe that all the Bible is necessary. Such an example tells him that some parts of the Bible are critical while others are not. How can a sinner know which parts are important and which are not? He cannot. He will instead simply lose interest in such an uninteresting and unconvincing witness.

Every Christian should be capable of rightly dividing the Word of God to every man. He should be able to discuss sensibly the subjects of repentance; forgiveness; baptism in Jesus' name; the indwelling of the Holy Ghost; the gifts of the Spirit; the Second Coming of Christ; the Rapture of the church; holiness; brotherly love; Heaven; hell; the devil; and the Godhead. If one does not study toward such an end, the result may be: he will not be "approved unto God", or he will eventually be "ashamed." He who studies well, and studies all the Word of God, will "be ready always to give an answer to every man that asketh you a reason of the hope that is in you" (I Peter 3:15).

A Final Word About Dogma and Doctrine

The nature of religion lends itself to dogmatism. One's religious beliefs carry eternal consequences. Therefore, one is far more likely to become dogmatic about his religious beliefs than any other ideology.

The basic difference between dogma and doctrine is not easy to define. Perhaps the best explanation would be to say that doctrine implies the acceptance of a belief taught by a church, while dogma implies a doctrine that is laid down as being true and beyond dispute.

The doctrines of salvation are beyond dispute, but the use of dogma sometimes deals with teaching doctrines for which there is no scriptural proof, yet declaring them to be beyond dispute. Jesus criticized the Pharisees for such practices: "Howbeit in vain do they worship me, teaching for doctrines the commandments of men" (Mark 7:7).

Proof that the early churches were in danger of adopting similar habits is found in Paul's admonition to the Colossians: "Wherefore if ye be dead with Christ from the rudiments of the world, why, as though living in the world, are ye subject to ordinances. . .after the commandments and doctrines of men?" (Colossians 2:20-22).

To make an absurd example, suppose a lady felt it was sinful to wear dresses which had polka dots. If to be true to her conviction she never wore such dresses, that would be a fine thing. However, if she began to teach other ladies that they could not be saved if they wore polka-dot dresses, then she would be teaching a personal dogma rather than declaring all the counsel of God, for there is not one verse in the Bible to substantiate such an idea.

The best safeguard against declaring wrong dogmas instead of true doctrines is study. Let every Christian understand that God wants him to be a declarer of the Word; and let him declare all the counsel of God, rightly dividing to every man his portion.

Test Your Knowledge

True or False

_____ 1. "Rightly dividing" implies that parts of the Bible are no longer relevant to modern Christianity.

_____ 2. There is only one way to declare God's Word.

_____ 3. There is a joy that comes in declaring the Word of God.

_____ 4. The ultimate purpose of declaring God's Word is to effect a change in the destiny of the hearer.

_____ 5. Good intentions without a plan, aim, or goal usually end in frustration.

_____ 6. If God's Word is declared to the world, it will be by people like you.

_____ 7. Paul's imprisonment kept him from declaring God's Word.

_____ 8. We should study God's Word that we may be able to "rightly divide" it.

_____ 9. If one knows how to "rightly divide" God's Word, there are appropriate passages of Scripture for every trial and situation.

_____10. One's religious beliefs carry eternal consequences.

Apply Your Knowledge

For each of the following circumstances, find two passages of Scripture which could edify, comfort and challenge the believer who is tried and tested.

Death in the family	Terminal illness
Loss of employment	Flat tire on automobile
Pain	Loneliness
Home lost in fire	Depression
Sickness	Anger

Utilizing again the principles learned in chapter seven, commit these passages to memory. By doing this, you will be ready always to offer a word of encouragement and hope when you encounter those who are hurting.

Expand Your Knowledge

Write your personal testimony on paper and entitle it, "Why I Believe God's Word." It is sometimes good to voice our appreciation for God and His Word. By expressing our testimony of faith, we become strengthened in that faith.

Believing the Word   10

> *"But this I confess unto thee, that after the way which they call heresy, so worship I the God of my fathers, believing all things which are written in the law and in the prophets."*
>
> Acts 24:14

Start with the Scriptures

Psalm 119:128
Mark 16:15-18
John 7:38-39; 20:31

Romans 1:16; 10:4-17
Hebrews 4:2

The Necessity of Believing the Word

Since the Word of God contains the message of salvation (John 5:39; 6:68), it is imperative that we receive, understand, and believe the Word. The Bible describes the new birth experience as "receiving the Word." Immediately after Cornelius and his household believed Peter's preaching, received the Holy Ghost, and received water baptism in Jesus' name the Bible records, "And the apostles and brethren that were in Judaea heard that the Gentiles had also received the word of God" (Acts 11:1).

In order to receive the Word in our lives, we must understand it. The Ethiopian eunuch was reading the Bible when Philip met him, but he did not understand what he read. After Philip explained the Scriptures to him, the eunuch understood the Word and was able to believe, confess, be baptized in water, and receive a joyous experience (Acts 8:27-39).

Not only must we understand the Word of God in order to experience salvation, we must believe it. Even though the Israelites in the wilderness had God's Word, most did not enter the Promised Land because they did not believe. This example admonishes us. "For unto us was the gospel preached, as well as unto them: but the word preached did not profit them, not being mixed with faith in them that heard it" (Hebrews 4:2).

The way to believe and worship God truly is to believe His Word. "Believe in the LORD your God, so shall ye be established; believe his prophets, so shall ye prosper" (II Chronicles 20:20).

In short, God gave us the Bible that we might believe its message and be saved. "I am not ashamed of the gospel of Christ: for it is the power of God unto salvation to every one that believeth" (Romans 1:16). "Thou hast known the holy scriptures, which are able to make thee wise unto salvation through faith which is in Christ Jesus" (II Timothy 3:15). "But these are written, that ye might believe that Jesus is the Christ, the Son of God; and that believing ye might have life through his name" (John 20:31).

What Is True Belief?

According to *Webster's Dictionary*, *belief* is "a

state or habit of mind in which trust or confidence is placed in some person or thing" and *faith* is "allegiance to duty or a person; loyalty. . .belief and trust in and loyalty to God. . .something that is believed esp. with strong conviction." The publisher's foreword to *The Amplified Bible* defines *believe* (Greek, *pisteuo*) as follows: "It means 'to adhere to, trust, to have faith in; to rely on.' Consequently, the words, 'Believe on the Lord Jesus Christ. . .' really mean to have an absolute personal reliance upon the Lord Jesus Christ as Saviour."

Vine's *Expository Dictionary of New Testament Words* says *pisteuo* means "to believe, also to be persuaded of, and hence, to place confidence in, to trust, signifies, in this sense of the word, reliance upon, not mere credence" (p. 118). It defines *belief* or *faith* (Greek, *pistis*) as "primarily, firm persuasion, a conviction based upon hearing. . . .The main elements in faith in its relation to the invisible God, as distinct from faith in man, are especially brought out in the use of this noun and the corresponding verb, *pisteuo*; they are (1) a firm conviction, producing a full acknowledgement of God's revelation or truth; e.g., II Thessalonians 2:11-12; (2) a personal surrender to Him, John 1:12; (3) a conduct inspired by such surrender, II Corinthians 5:7. . .All this stands in contrast to belief in its purely natural exercise, which consists of an opinion held in good faith without necessary reference to its proof" (p. 411).

In other words, saving faith means much more than mental knowledge or assent. In fact, we can identify three key components of saving faith: knowledge, assent, and appropriation.

First, to have faith in something, one must have a certain degree of knowledge or mental understanding. He must know what he professes to believe. Saving faith does not require us to understand everything about God or life, but we must realize our need of salvation and know that Jesus Christ is our only Savior.

Second, to have faith there must be assent or mental acceptance. Knowledge is not enough, for one can understand a certain proposition and yet disbelieve it. In addition to understanding, there must be an acknowledgement that the profession is correct.

Finally, there must be an appropriation or application of truth. We do this by obeying the gospel of Jesus Christ, by identifying with Him, by totally committing ourselves to Him, by establishing a relationship of total trust in, adherence to, and reliance upon Him.

The Scriptures give many examples of those who had some degree of faith in Christ but were not saved. (See Matthew 7:21-27; John 2:23-25; 12:42-43; Acts 8:18-23; James 2:19.) Thus one can have a mental belief in Jesus as Lord and Savior and yet not obey Him, rely upon Him or commit oneself to Him to the point of salvation.

A number of scriptural passages emphasize that obedience is an essential aspect of saving faith. The mystery of God's redemptive plan, the church, has been "made known to all nations for the obedience of faith" (Romans 16:26). God's grace brings "obedience to the faith" (Romans 1:5). Christ worked through Paul to "make the Gentiles obedient" (Romans 15:18). A great number of priests were "obedient to the faith" (Acts 6:7). Many other passages stress the necessity of obedience to the Word of God (John 14:15, 23; II Thessalonians 1:7-10; Hebrews 5:9; I Peter 4:17; I John 2:3-5; 5:1-3).

When God sent the death angel to visit every household in Egypt, the Israelites were not automatically protected simply on the basis of their mental attitude. They had to apply the blood of the passover lamb to their doorposts (Exodus 12). Only when they expressed their faith through obedience in God's command were they safe.

Theologian Dietrich Bonhoeffer said, "Only he who believes is obedient, and only he who is obedient believes."

The Application or Expression of True Belief

Exactly what will faith in the Word of God produce? Jesus preached, "Repent ye, and believe the gospel" (Mark 1:15). One must have some faith in order to repent. No one seeks to repent from sin unless he believes that sin is wrong and that repentance is both possible and necessary. God's Word declares that without repentance all will perish and that all men everywhere must repent (Luke 13:3; Acts 17:30). Certainly, then, faith in the Word of God will lead to repentance. Repentance is the first faith response to God.

Faith in God will also lead to water baptism. Jesus said, "He that believeth and is baptized shall be saved" (Mark 16:16). Obviously He taught that faith would lead to baptism, and the history of the Early Church affirms this truth. After Peter's sermon on the Day of Pentecost, "they that gladly received his word were baptized" (Acts 2:41). When the Samaritans "believed Philip preaching the things concerning the kingdom of God, and the name of Jesus Christ, they were baptized" (Acts 8:12). The Philippian jailer believed and was baptized in the same hour that Paul admonished him to believe (Acts 16:31-34). When Paul preached in Corinth, many people "believed, and were baptized" (Acts 18:8). We conclude that water baptism is an act of faith—a faith response to God. True faith in God and His Word will cause the believer to receive water baptism.

Faith also leads to receiving the gift of the Holy Ghost. Jesus said, "He that believeth on me, as the scripture hath said, out of his belly shall flow rivers of living water'' (John 7:38). John explained, "But this spake he of the Spirit, which they that believe on him should receive: for the Holy Ghost was not yet given; because that Jesus was not yet glorified'' (John 7:39).

Peter taught that the gift, or baptism, of the Holy Ghost comes to all who believe on the Lord Jesus Christ. He identified Cornelius' experience as the same Holy Spirit baptism as was received at Pentecost and asked, "Forasmuch then as God gave them the like gift as he did unto us, who believed on the Lord Jesus Christ; what was I, that I could withstand God?'' (Acts 11:17).

Paul also expected that believers would receive the Holy Ghost. When he found some disciples of John the Baptist at Ephesus he asked, "Have ye received the Holy Ghost since ye believed?'' (Acts 19:2). Paul further taught in his epistles that we receive the Holy Spirit through faith. "That the blessing of Abraham might come on the Gentiles through Jesus Christ; that we might receive the promise of the Spirit through faith'' (Galatians 3:14).

Faith in God will always generate a holy lifestyle and good works. "This is a faithful saying, and these things I will that thou affirm constantly, that they which have believed in God might be careful to maintain good works'' (Titus 3:8). "Faith, if it hath not works, is dead, being alone'' (James 2:17). Saving faith will produce a life-changing reliance upon God, evidenced by works. We are saved through faith; but saving faith will always produce works and can only be demonstrated by works (James 2:14-26).

Thus, saving faith results in repentance, water baptism in Jesus' name, receiving the Holy Ghost, and living a holy life filled with good works.

Belief, Confession, and Salvation

Does this conclusion about saving faith contradict Romans 10? "The word is nigh thee, even in thy mouth, and in thy heart: that is, the word of faith, which we preach; That if thou shalt confess with thy mouth the Lord Jesus, and shalt believe in thine heart that God hath raised him from the dead, thou shalt be saved. For with the heart man believeth unto righteousness; and with the mouth confession is made unto salvation. . . .For whosoever shall call upon the name of the Lord shall be saved" (Romans 10:8-10, 13).

Some interpret this passage to mean that salvation comes automatically if a person mentally assents that Jesus rose from the dead and verbally confesses that He is Lord; however, this interpretation contradicts the truth that saving faith includes appropriation and obedience.

Many people might verbally confess Jesus as Lord and call on His name but will not actually be saved because they do not obey His will (Matthew 7:21-23). Even the devils know Jesus is alive, confess Him verbally, and believe in one God (Matthew 8:29; James 2:19). A superficial reading of Romans 10 is inadequate.

To understand this passage correctly a person must look at the context. Paul was not telling sinners how to be saved, but was writing to Christians, reminding them of the accessibility and availability of salvation to all. We do not have to go up to heaven or across the sea to find out what the Word of God or the will of God is; it is the same word we have already learned and are speaking (Deuteronomy 30:12-14, quoted in Romans 10:6-8). Salvation is available to all who will turn to God, both Jew and Gentile (Romans 10:12).

Paul's hearers had already experienced the new

birth; he simply reminded them that to keep their salvation and to receive eternal salvation in the future they needed to keep believing and confessing.

Deuteronomy 30:14 (quoted in Romans 10:8) states, "But the word is very nigh unto thee, in thy mouth, and in thy heart, that thou mayest do it." This demonstrates that confessing and believing always includes obedience. Romans 10:16 likewise indicates that a lack of obedience is a lack of faith: "But they have not all obeyed the gospel. For Esaias saith, Lord, who hath believed our report?"

To "confess with thy mouth the Lord Jesus" means to give a truthful, verbal confession that Jesus is Lord. For this to be truthful, we must submit our lives to Him as Lord and obey Him.

When do we first confess Jesus as Lord? Verbal confession comes when we call His name at water baptism (Acts 22:16) and when we speak in tongues at the Spirit baptism (Acts 2:4). No one can confess that Jesus is Lord except by the Holy Spirit (I Corinthians 12:3). In the fullest sense, no one can truly confess Jesus as Lord of his life until he receives the Spirit and lives by the Spirit's power.

To "believe in thy heart that God has raised him [Christ] from the dead" means to believe in the resurrection and rely upon its message and experience for salvation. We rely on the resurrection to make Christ's atoning death effective (Romans 4:21-25) and to give us new life through the Spirit of the risen Christ (Romans 5:10; 6:4-5; 8:9-11). True belief in Christ's resurrection will lead us to apply His atonement to our lives and specifically to receive His Spirit.

To "call upon the name of the Lord" for salvation describes the sincere cry of the repentant believer. Oral confession is a step in that direction, but living faith and obedience are required to validate this confession. Paul quoted this phrase from Joel 2:32. It follows Joel's prophecy concerning the latter-day outpouring of the Spirit and the latter-day judgment of God (verses 28-31), and Peter applied it to the outpouring of the Spirit at Pentecost (Acts 2:21). Also, calling on the Lord's name occurs at baptism (Acts 22:16).

Believing All the Word

As this discussion has indicated, we should believe and obey *all* the Word. Some critics maintain that the Bible contains the Word of God, but that all parts of the Bible are not necessarily true. Some people try to explain away the miracles recorded in Scripture, while others do not believe all the historical accounts in the Bible. Some of the greatest enemies of God's Word today are those who use historical-critical methods of interpretation to reject biblical statements and teachings.

Jesus said God's Word is truth (John 17:17), and therefore it cannot contain error. All Scripture, not just a part of Scripture, is given by inspiration of God (literally, "God-breathed") and is profitable for doctrine, reproof, correction, and instruction in righteousness (II Timothy 3:16).

For Scripture to fulfill this divine purpose it cannot contain error. Thus, the Bible in its entirety is the inerrant Word of God. If any error exists in a particular copy of the Bible, it is due to the mistake of a copyist, translator, or printer, not to the original process of inspiration.

The psalmist confessed his belief that the Law was wholly correct. "Therefore I esteem all thy precepts concerning all things to be right" (Psalm 119:128). Jesus and the apostles believed the Old Testament fully and quoted it often. In particular, they endorsed many passages most attacked by critics, such as the accounts of Adam and Eve and of Jonah. They based important doctrinal truths on historical details, such as finding important typology concerning Christ in the stories of Jonah and Melchizedek (Matthew 12:40; Hebrews 7). In all, the New Testament quotes from, refers to, or describes events from all books in the original Hebrew canon except two small ones (Esther and Song of Solomon). Paul confessed belief in everything written in the law and prophets (Acts 24:14).

If we believe all the Word we will not only accept biblical miracles but miracles today. Mark 16:17-18 promises believers that they can have such miraculous signs as power over demons, speaking in tongues, divine protection from accidental harm, and divine healing. If we believe all the Word, we should apply all of its teachings to our lives.

The Bible contains numerous examples of people who believed and stood fast on the Word of God. Hebrews 11 lists many of them, stating, "These all died in faith, not having received the promises, but having seen them afar off, and were persuaded of them, and embraced them" (Hebrews 11:13). If we wish to be saved and to see God's work in our lives, we too must stand on the Word—we must receive, understand, believe, and obey the Word of God.

Test Your Knowledge

1. Since the Word of God contains the message of _____, it is imperative that we receive, understand and believe the Word.

2. In order to receive the Word in our lives, we must _____ it.

3. The Ethiopian eunuch was reading the _____ when Philip met him.

4. The way to believe and worship God truly is to _____ His Word.

5. Saving faith is much more than mental _____ or _____.

6. _____ is an essential aspect of saving faith.

7. We apply the blood of the Lamb to our lives by _____ to His _____.

8. _____ leads to receiving the gift of the Holy Ghost.

9. Faith in God will always generate a _____ lifestyle and good _____.

10. _____ and believing always include obedience.

Apply Your Knowledge

Write a brief summary essay on "What Constitutes Saving Faith." In this essay you should explain how believing and faith work together in our lives to motivate us to obedience of the Scriptures and a holy lifestyle. Even though we are not saved by works, they maintain a very vital place of importance in a Christian's life. Explain this also.

Writing out this assignment will help you to fully understand this chapter and the important concepts it covers.

Expand Your Knowledge

Find a verse or passage of Scripture in the New Testament which shows the fulfillment of the following prophecies of Christ from the Old Testament:
Isaiah 53:3—Rejection by Jews
Psalm 22:16—Pierced in hands and feet
Psalm 69:21—Given gall and vinegar
Psalm 22:18—Lots cast for garments
Psalm 34:20—Bones not broken
Psalm 16:10—Resurrection
Psalm 68:18—Ascension

11 Proving the Word

"Prove all things; hold fast that which is good."
I Thessalonians 5:21

Start with the Scriptures

Deuteronomy 13:1-11; 18:20-22
Isaiah 8:14-20; 41:21-23; 44:6-8; 45:21-23; 46:9-11
Malachi 3:10

Throughout this study we have assumed the Bible to be the Word of God. What ground do we have for making this assumption? How can we be certain this is correct?

The Bible itself bids us to investigate and prove the truth for ourselves and to be prepared to explain the basis of our faith to others. "Prove all things; hold fast that which is good" (I Thessalonians 5:21).

Those who believe in God should expect Him to communicate with mankind. If He was interested enough to create man, surely He is interested enough to communicate with man. If He is our Father, surely He wishes to have a relationship with His children. If He is a God of love and mercy, surely He cares enough to help sinful, hurting man.

From our belief in an intelligent, loving Creator, we should expect to find the Word of God among men. How can we know where to find His Word? There is convincing evidence that the Bible is the unique Word of God to man. We will discuss twenty points of proof under six major headings.

The Bible's Own Testimony

Unique claims of the Bible. We would certainly expect the Word of God to identify itself as such, and the Bible does indeed claim to be the inspired, infallible Word of God (II Timothy 3:16; II Peter 1:21). Each book of the Bible claims, either directly or indirectly, to be God's Word. Of all the books of the world's great religions, only one other book boasts of equal authority—the Koran of the Moslems—and its fanciful content does not support its claim. If we find the Bible to be trustworthy (for reasons discussed below), then we should accept its own testimony about itself.

Self-vindicating authority. The Bible speaks with such authority and power that its inspiration is self-evident. Those who heard Jesus teach recognized that He spoke with unique authority like that of no other man (Mark 1:22; John 7:46). Likewise, we recognize the unique authority of the Bible when we read it. It actually needs no defense; it speaks for itself.

Testimony of the prophets and apostles. The prophets and apostles who wrote the Scriptures testified that they spoke not of themselves but by the Spirit of God. The men of God in every age accepted earlier biblical books as divinely inspired. For example, the Old Testament kings and prophets accepted the books of Moses as the Word of God, and the New Testament writers accepted the Old Testament as Scripture.

Integrity of Jesus Christ. Jesus Christ accepted the entire Old Testament as God's Word (Luke 24:44-45). He commissioned the writers of the New Testament to proclaim His gospel to the world and promised that God's Spirit would lead them into all truth (Matthew 28:19-20; John 16:13). To reject the Bible is to reject the authority of Christ.

One cannot accept Jesus as a man of integrity and yet reject the authority of the Scriptures. Either the Bible is the Word of God as Jesus claimed, or else Jesus was a liar, deceiver, or fool. If the Bible is not God's Word, then Jesus was not a noble and wise man, for such a man would not perpetrate the world's greatest hoax.

The Character of the Bible

Content. The Bible teaches us about God, man, sin, salvation, judgment, and eternity. It deals with man's deepest spiritual questions and aspirations. Certainly we would expect the Word of God to handle such subjects, and the Bible does so in an exalted fashion unequaled by any other book.

Moral superiority. The Bible teaches us about holiness, morality, love, justice, truth, and mercy in a way that no other book does. No other religion or book so totally identifies God with love. No other ancient religion or book has the Bible's unique emphasis on strict monotheism and on ethical conduct. The Bible contains the highest moral teachings of any book in the world. The world's most moral book would not proclaim the world's biggest lie; if it were not the Word of God it would not claim to be so.

Unity. The Bible was written by approximately forty different writers from widely divergent backgrounds over 1600 years, yet it has one doctrinal system. Unlike the scriptures of other major religions, it is unified. It teaches one morality, one basic plan of salvation, and one program for the future.

Alternative possibilities. If the Bible is not God's Word, what could be? None of the world's great books compare in morality and content. Furthermore, if the Bible is not God's Word, who created it? Good men or angels would not falsely claim divine inspiration, and evil men or angels would not teach such high morality.

Historical and Scientific Verification

Agreement with history. Research has confirmed numerous historical accounts in the Scriptures, from the patriarchal period to the Israelites in Egypt, to the conquest of Canaan, to the kingdom of Solomon, to the Babylonian captivity. Traditions from many lands agree with the biblical account of Noah's flood. Scholars once scoffed at biblical references to the Hittites because no secular source mentioned them, until twentieth-century excavations in Turkey proved the existence of an ancient and powerful Hittite empire. A Moabite stone inscription describes the very battle mentioned in II Kings 3. Archives of ancient Egypt, Assyria, and Babylonia have verified many biblical incidents as well as biblical names of kings, generals, pharaohs, and emperors. Archeologists have long used the Bible to locate lost cities and wells.

Archaeology has proven the accuracy of biblical details such as the antiquity and genuineness of proper names in Genesis, legal and social customs of the patriarchs in Genesis, customs of the ancient

Egyptians in the story of Joseph, the water tunnel David used to conquer Jerusalem (II Samuel 5:8), Hezekiah's aqueduct (II Kings 20:20), the judgment seat where Jesus was tried (John 19:13), the temple of Diana at Ephesus (Acts 19:27), and much more. For years scholars were puzzled by the unusual Greek of the New Testament, until discovery of ancient papyri proved that the New Testament was written in the commoner's dialect of the first century.

Agreement with science. Although many superstitions and false scientific concepts existed in Bible days, the Bible never contradicts true science. How could such an ancient book avoid the many gross misconceptions of its time unless it were divinely inspired?

The geological record of sedimentary deposits and fossils supports the biblical account of a universal, cataclysmic flood. Mathematicians value the number pi, which represents the circumference of a circle divided by its diameter, at approximately 3.14, and II Chronicles 4:2 gives the close approximation of 3.

The Bible sometimes alludes to scientific truths unknown to ancient man, such as the life-sustaining role of blood (Genesis 9:4; Leviticus 17:14), the earth hanging in outer space (Job 26:7), and the roundness of the earth (Isaiah 40:22).

Witness in Human Society

Indestructibility. Men have transmitted the Bible over thousands of years, relying on handwritten copies throughout most of history. Furthermore, as the discovery of the Dead Sea Scrolls demonstrated, the text of the Scriptures has been preserved with incredible accuracy unequaled by any other ancient book.

In addition, the Bible has withstood centuries of

attack by its enemies, from Roman attempts to destroy it physically to medieval attempts to ban it from the masses to atheistic attempts to discredit it and prove it false. Only divine providence could have preserved the Bible under these conditions.

Universality. We would probably expect God to seek the widest possible distribution of His Word to mankind. The Bible is the most universal book in the world in terms of applicability, translation, and distribution. Portions of the Bible have been translated in over 1100 languages and dialects, representing ninety percent of the world's population. An estimated two billion Bibles have been distributed throughout history. (See Norman Geisler and William Nix, *A General Introduction to the Bible,* Chicago: Moody Press, 1968.) There are no close seconds; the distant seconds are books related to the Bible, such as *Pilgrim's Progress* and *The Imitation of Christ.*

Influence on society. No other book has enriched human society as much as the Bible has. The Bible has inspired much of the world's finest music, sculpture, painting, architecture, and literature. The Bible has influenced the fundamental laws of many nations and has motivated many of the world's greatest social reforms, such as the abolition of slavery. No other book can claim anything like the ennobling, spiritual impact the Bible has had on human society.

Witness in Individual Lives

Witness of the Spirit. The Holy Spirit confirms to us individually that the Bible is the Word of God. When we believe and obey the Bible, God's Spirit bears witness to our spirits that we are God's children by regeneration (Romans 8:16).

Life-changing power. The Bible changes the lives

of those who believe and obey its teachings. Individuals are converted supernaturally, souls are regenerated, people are delivered from sinful habits, addictions, and lifestyles, and sinners are transformed into saints.

Fulfilled promises and miracles. When people apply the Bible to their lives, miracles occur. People speak in tongues just like the Bible teaches. Supernatural healings take place, and demonic powers are expelled. God answers the prayers of those who pray in accordance with the Bible. In fact, the Bible challenges us to claim its promises and see if they are true. In Malachi 3:10, God asked His people to prove Him by paying tithes and waiting for the promised blessings to come to the nation.

Fullfilled Prophecy

The Bible is the only prophetic book of all the books of major religions. It is the only book containing many specific predictions that have actually come to pass. The Bible asks us to test its truth by comparing its prophetic accuracy with that of other religions.

God challenged other religions to prove their case by describing the past and predicting the future accurately as He did: "Produce your cause, saith the LORD; bring forth your strong reasons, saith the King of Jacob. Let them bring them forth, and shew us what shall happen: let them shew the former things, what they be, that we may consider them, and know the latter end of them; or declare us things for to come. Shew the things that are to come hereafter, that we may know that ye are gods" (Isaiah 41:21-23). (See also Isaiah 44:6-8; 45:21.) God promises that His Word will surely come to pass (Isaiah 45:23; 46:9-11).

Someone has estimated that one fourth of all

verses in the Bible are predictive, with 1,183 events predicted literally and 634 events predicted symbolically. Even without using symbolic, figurative, or typological predictions, many literal prophecies have already come to pass just as the Bible foretold. The following are some examples of fulfilled prophecy.

Fulfilled prophecies concerning Israel. The Bible records many specific prophecies that have come to pass, including a prediction naming King Josiah 340 years in advance (I Kings 13:2; II Kings 23:15-16) and the prediction about Queen Jezebel's death (I Kings 21:23; II Kings 9:36). Many prophecies about Israel have been fulfilled in exact detail.

The Bible prophesied that Israel would be dispersed (Deuteronomy 28:15-68; Jeremiah 15:4; 16:13; Hosea 3:4). The northern kingdom of Israel and its capital Samaria would be overthrown permanently but Judah would be preserved (I Kings 14:15; Isaiah 7:6-9; Hosea 1:6; Micah 1:6-9). Judah and Jerusalem would escape Assyrian conquest but would fall to the Babylonians (Isaiah 39:6; Jeremiah 25:9-12). The Medes and Persians would overthrow Babylon (Isaiah 21:2; Daniel 5:28), and the city and Temple of Jerusalem would be restored through the edict of Cyrus, who was named 176 years before the event (Isaiah 44:28; 45:1; Jeremiah 29:10-14). Israel would be regathered (Isaiah 11:11).

Fulfilled prophecies concerning Gentile nations. Examples are the futures of Babylon, Tyre, Egypt, Ammon, Moab, Edom, and Philistia (Isaiah 13-23; Jeremiah 46-51), the destruction of Tyre (Ezekiel 26), the judgment of Petra in Edom (Obadiah 1-4), and the emergence of the four great empires: Babylon, Medo-Persia, Greece, Rome (Daniel 2, 7). Daniel 11 describes the conflict between Syria and Egypt in such great detail and with such accuracy that liberal scholars claim the book must have been written after this time.

Fulfilled prophecies concerning Jesus the Messiah. The Old Testament predicted, among other things, Christ's lineage from Judah and David, miraculous conception, Galilean ministry, rejection by the Jews, time of birth, place of birth, triumphal entry into Jerusalem, and betrayal for thirty pieces of silver (Genesis 49:10; Isaiah 7:14; 9:1-2; 11:1; 53:3; Daniel 9:25; Micah 5:2; Zechariah 9:9; 11:12).

The Bible predicted many details of Christ's trial and death, including the silence of Christ when accused, smiting and spitting, punishment with criminals, piercing of hands and feet, mockery, offering of gall and vinegar, casting of lots for His garments, bones of His body not broken, burial with the rich, resurrection, and ascension (Psalm 16:10; 22:6-8, 16-18; 34:20; 68:18; 69:21; Isaiah 50:6; 53:1-12; Zechariah 12:10).

Fulfilled prophecies concerning the latter days. Many latter-day prophecies have already been fulfilled partially or totally, such as the restoration of Israel (Ezekiel 37), increase of knowledge and travel (Daniel 12:4), outpouring of the Spirit (Joel 2:28), destruction of the Temple (Matthew 24:1-2), continuance and increase of false christs, wars, rumors of wars, famines, pestilences, earthquakes, persecution, false prophets, and backsliding (Matthew 24:4-12), preservation of a remnant of Israel (Romans 11:5, 25), and increase of wickedness (II Timothy 3:1-13).

The Test of True Prophecy

Having established the Bible as the Word of God, we can use it to test all other messages claiming divine inspiration or approval. Indeed, the Bible commands us to judge all prophecies and to test all spirits (I Corinthians 14:29; I John 4:1). The Bible gives the following tests of true prophecy.

True prophecy will always affirm the worship of the one true God. If a prophet, dreamer, or miracle worker teaches the people to go after other gods, he is false (Deuteronomy 13:1-11). Only false prophets will seek counsel from mediums, spiritists, witches, or wizards instead of God (Isaiah 8:19-20).

True prophecy will always conform to the teaching of the Scriptures. Only false prophets will contradict God's law (Isaiah 8:20). If a man or an angel preaches any other gospel he is accursed (Galatians 1:8-9). Any spirit that refuses to confess the incarnation of Jesus Christ is antichrist (I John 4:3).

If a prophecy does not come to pass it is not of God (Deuteronomy 18:20-22).

Every book of the Bible conforms to these standards, and so will all truth proclaimed by godly preachers today.

The evidence testifies overwhelmingly to the divine inspiration, supreme authority, and infallibility of the Bible as the Word of God. The Bible itself testifies to its unique status, and to reject its claims is to reject the authority of Jesus Christ.

We can demonstrate its inspiration by an analysis of its character, by historical and scientific verification, and by its impact upon human society. We can also prove the Bible by applying it to our own lives and experiencing its dynamic power personally. Finally, the fulfilled prophecies of the Scriptures are an amazing testimony to its supernatural character.

God has challenged us to prove His Word; when we do we will find it to be true in every way. The Bible then becomes the standard of truth by which we measure all things. Once we have proved and tested the Word of God for ourselves, we can wield it as "the sword of the Spirit" (Ephesians 6:17). With this invincible weapon we can vanquish all foes—unbelief, temptation, sin, and Satan himself.

Test Your Knowledge

Give the Scripture references:

1. _____ "Prove all things; hold fast that which is good."
2. _____ "Be ready always to give an answer to every man that asketh you a reason of the hope that is in you with meekness and fear."
3. _____ "All Scripture is given by inspiration of God, and is profitable for doctrine, for reproof, for correction, for instruction in righteousness."
4. _____ "The Spirit itself beareth witness with our spirit, that we are the children of God."
5. _____ "But though we, or an angel from heaven, preach any other gospel unto you than that which we have preached unto you, let him be accursed."

Apply Your Knowledge

Find and list at least ten verses of Scripture which declare the correctness, authority, or infallibility of God's Word. We can rest assured in God's Word for it has stood the test of time and truth.

Expand Your Knowledge

Read the Scriptures located under "Start With the Scriptures" for the following chapter. This will better prepare you for the study that follows.

Applying the Word   12

"For the word of God is quick, and powerful, and sharper than any two-edged sword, piercing even to the dividing asunder of soul and spirit, and of the joints and marrow, and is a discerner of the thoughts and intents of the heart."

Hebrews 4:12

Start with the Scriptures

Romans 3:10, 23; 5:1-8, 12; 6:23
Ephesians 5:6
II Timothy 3:16
James 1:22-25

The Importance of Applying the Word

A distinction should be made between hearing the Word and applying the Word. There are far more hearers than there are those who apply what they have heard.

James referred to those in the latter category as "doers of the Word," and he offered insight into the distinction between the two when he wrote, "But be ye doers of the word, and not hearers only, deceiving your own selves. For if any be a hearer of the word, and not a doer, he is like unto a man beholding his natural face in a glass: For he beholdeth himself, and goeth his way, and straightway forgetteth what manner of man he was. But whoso looketh into the perfect law of liberty, and continueth therein, he being not a forgetful hearer, but a doer of the work, this man shall be blessed in his deed" (James 1:22-25).

Important reasons exist for applying the Word of God, and they cannot be overstated.

Salvation. James wrote that we should "receive with meekness the engrafted word, which is able to save your souls" (James 1:21). The engrafted Word is the applied Word. A person should not expect to be saved just because he has heard the Word, whether he has heard one sermon or a thousand. He must apply the Word he has heard if it is going to benefit him and save him. He should obey it. It must be engrafted, and he must become a doer of the Word of God in order for salvation to be his.

Understanding true doctrine. All doctrines claim to be based on the Word of God and yet not all doctrines are true. Can they all be right and yet be so different? Of course not. Some doctrines are true, and some are false. Study alone does not guarantee that one will find the truth and recognize the false, for many people have devoted their lives to the study of the Word yet still preach and practice wrong doctrines. If study alone does not lead one into the truth, what does?

One must be wiling to study the Word of God for reasons other than the proving of a point, or a doctrine. Men who are spiritually blind abound with theories, and when they study they are studying to prove their points. But the proper motive for studying the Word is a desire to know God and to please Him. A person should lay aside his personal ideas.

To understand true doctrine is to understand God. When one reads the Bible with the desire to discover what God wants of him, then his chances of discovering truth are great. The willingness to apply whatever one finds in the Scriptures is the best assurance that a person has of understanding true doctrine.

Overcoming temptations. The psalmist wrote, "Thy word have I hid in mine heart, that I might not sin against thee" (Psalm 119:11). It is through an understanding of the Word of God that a person overcomes temptations to sin. Perhaps the writer was wishing he might have had more of God's Word in his heart at an earlier time in his life when he wrote those words. Perhaps he realized that there might not have been an adulterous affair and a murder on his record if he could have had more of God's Word in his heart.

Jesus, at the beginning of His ministry, was tempted of Satan in the wilderness. In response to Satan's temptations, Jesus remarked, "It is written, Man shall not live by bread alone, but by every word that proceedeth out of the mouth of God" (Matthew 4:4).

If Jesus Christ, who as God could have snapped His fingers and called angels to His rescue, chose instead to overcome the evil one by quoting verses of Scripture, does it not make sense that He did it as an example to show us that the way to overcome is through the Word of God?

Instruction in righteous living. It is assumed that every true Christian wants to live a sinless life after Christ's pattern. How can we know for sure what God expects of us? It is discovering His will in His Word. He inspired men to write that we might profit by it. "All scripture is given by inspiration of God, and is profitable for doctrine, for reproof, for correction, for instruction in righteousness: That the man of God may be perfect, throughly furnished unto all good works" (II Timothy 3:16).

The only way a person can be sure he is living the right life, doing the right works, is through understanding and applying the Word of God.

Incentives for Applying the Word

Exciting things begin to happen in the lives of those who begin to apply the Word of God to their lives. Doers of the Word soon discover new dimensions of life opening up to them. We can notice what Jesus said to Satan in the wilderness: "Man shall not live by bread alone, but by every word that proceedeth out of the mouth of God" (Matthew 4:4). A man may exist on bread, but if he wants to live—to really live and know life at its best—he must find it in the Word of God.

Living life at its best. Jesus said, "I am come that they might have life, and that they might have it more abundantly" (John 10:10). How do we receive that life from Him? "The words that I speak unto you, they are spirit, and they are life" (John 6:63).

Abundant life is found by applying the Word of God to our lives.

Those individuals who live by this world's values are always seeking the happy life, the rich life. Their psychiatrists, psychologists, analysts, and counselors are forever trying to find the key to happiness and fulfillment for them, but their pursuit carries them down a primrose path. Personal pleasure and self-acceptance become their goal.

There is likely a place in society for pscyhologists and psychiatrists, but too often their remedies are mere Band-Aids for wounds that need surgery. They often take the money of the brokenhearted, but only offer a pat on the back and an understanding nod. They rearrange the chains of bondage upon the "captive," but he is still bound when he leaves their offices.

Jesus Christ does not offer a temporary soothing, but a permanent cure. He said, "The Spirit of the Lord is upon me, because he hath anointed me to preach the gospel to the poor; he hath sent me to heal the brokenhearted, to preach deliverance to the captives, and recovering of sight to the blind, to set at liberty them that are bruised" (Luke 4:18).

Salvation. Salvation has already been mentioned in this chapter, but it must be mentioned again. What greater incentive could anyone have than the saving of his own soul? James wrote that it was the applied Word that was "able to save your souls" (James 1:21). Even if there were no promise of joy in serving God, the knowledge that a man is saved ought to be incentive enough to cause him to want to obey the Word of the Lord.

Healing. "He sent his word, and healed them" (Psalm 107:20). In Matthew 8:8, a centurion knew that his servant who was ill could be healed if Jesus would simply "speak the word only." We have His Word in written form, and if it is applied, all of its promises belong to us. "Is any sick among you? let him call for the elders of the church; and let them pray over him, anointing him with oil in the name of the Lord: And the prayer of faith shall save the sick, and the Lord shall raise him up; and if he have committed sins, they shall be forgiven him" (James 5:14-15).

Power. Just before He was received up into heaven, Jesus promised a phenomenal, powerful experience to those who believed (Mark 16:15-18; Acts 1:8). After He vanished into the heavens, His disciples began to preach, and the Lord worked with them, confirming the Word of God with the signs He had just promised to those who believed (Mark 16:20). It is the Word that causes God to work in our midst. If we preach the Word and practice the

Word, we will know the power of God.

Keeps from error. The Sadducees in Jesus' day would certainly have claimed to know the Scriptures, yet on one occasion when they were questioning Jesus, He said to them, "Ye do err, not knowing the scriptures" (Matthew 22:29). They thought they knew them, but as has already been pointed out, to read them is not necessarily to know them.

A person must desire to know the Author and seek to please Him by finding His will in His Word. Had the Sadducees been willing to accept the Scriptures as pointing the way to Jesus Christ, instead of using them to reinforce their dead doctrines, they would not have erred. To know the Scriptures and to apply them to one's life, is to be kept from error.

Keeps from sin. Obeying the Word of God makes a person free from sin. "But God be thanked, that ye were the servants of sin, but ye have obeyed from the heart that form of doctrine which was delivered you. Being then made free from sin, ye became the servants of righteousness" (Romans 6:17-18).

Instructions for Applying the Word

Realizing the importance of applying the Word of God and having many incentives for applying it, the thing needed then is to know how to apply the Word. Two sets of instructions are offered here. The first set of instructions will help a person know how to apply the Word to himself; the second set will help him know how to apply it to others.

There seems to be an abundance of people who are able to tell others how to live, but never manage their own affairs well. Solomon, the wise king, said that he had kept the vineyards of others, but had not kept his own (Song of Solomon 1:6).

Most of us know someone who is full of advice, but whose own life is a chaotic mess. It is important, therefore, that the reader of the Bible understands that it is proper for him to read with the Bible in one hand and a mirror in the other.

The Bible's truths must be first applied to self, then they can be applied in teaching others. "Show me a sermon," one man cried. His message is clear—"Don't tell me what to do until I can see by your own habits that you practice what you preach." That is good counsel for all to follow.

The following are some suggestions for applying the Word to self.

Devote yourself to the Word. We need to learn to love it and to cradle it in careful hands. Most everyone has probably observed a man in a hospital corridor, taking his daily walk. He pushes before him some kind of a contraption on wheels. From that machine, hoses and wires run back to the man and are attached somehow to his body.

We do not have to know the name or the function of the machine to realize that the man's very life depends upon the success or failure of that machine. He is careful with it. He never tries to leave the machine in one place and take a walk without it. He holds on to it. He is careful in all his movements. He guards it well around corners lest some careless person run into it.

We can let the Bible be our machine. A Christian can attach it to himself with invisible cords of love. He should never try to go anywhere without taking it with him. His life rests in that Book. His success or failure depends upon whether he is applying that Book to himself.

Discipline yourself to read it. There is a difference in reading and studying. Because some people know the discipline study requires, they shy away from reading. A Christian, however, should beware of avoiding the Bible because he thinks he does not have time to read it.

Reading takes only as much time as a person wishes to give to it. It can be five minutes; it can be an hour. But a Christian should read.

A minister's son was privileged to be able to attend a renowned college in England. Though the father was proud for his son, he was also worried about the boy's consecration and feared that when he was away from his teaching, surrounded by important sounding professors, he might lose some of his faith in the Bible. Unable to be completely silent about the matter, in the days prior to his son's departure, the minister began to hint at his fear.

"Don't let them take the Book of Jonah away from you, Son," he joked, knowing that the Book of Jonah might well be singled out as literary fantasy. The boy tried to assure his father that his faith was secure, but the father's fear stayed with him.

When the first year of college was over and the son returned home for the summer, his father was anxious to find out how his son's faith had fared.

"Well, Son," he smiled nervously over supper, "tell me, did they take the Book of Jonah away from you?"

"Dad," the boy retorted, almost cynically, "You don't even have the Book of Jonah in your Bible." The father feared the worst, that his son had been convinced the Book was not accurate. But the boy arose, got his father's Bible, and offered it to him, repeating his challenge that the Book of Jonah was not even in his father's Bible.

Opening the Bible to show him the Book of Jonah, the father was shocked when he could not find it. His son handed him two pages, the Book of Jonah, which he had carefully cut with a razor blade from his father's Bible before he left for college over ten months before. His father had not known.

"Dad, what difference does it make if they try to teach it away? If we have it, but never read it, what is the difference?"

The son's point is well taken. What good is our Bible if we never read it? What good is it if we only read from it once a month? If the Bible really works for our benefit, and we have proven that it does, then why not get as much of it as we can?

Christians need to discipline themselves to read the Bible. Certain subjects often come up that we may wish to study seriously, but we should never confuse study with reading. A few minutes of Bible reading each day can go a long way toward teaching us how to live after Christ's pattern.

Determine to tell others about the Word. A Christian may not be ready to commit himself to telling someone daily about the Lord, but how about once a week? Could he determine that he would tell at least one person about the Lord between Monday and Saturday? If that seems too hard, then how about once a month? Even at that rate, a person would talk to twelve people in a year's time. Have we talked seriously to twelve people in the past year? If not, we should determine that we will improve in this area of applying the Word of the Lord.

Talking about the Word of God sharpens our skills in using it. Some people are denominational in their religion to the extent that they let the denomination work out their salvation. They cannot personally show in the Scriptures why they believe what they say they believe, but they will be quick to say their "church" believes it.

Some people have confessed that the best thing that ever happened to them concerning Bible study was to be embarrassed by someone who knew more about the Bible than they did. When someone of another doctrine seems to know more about the Scriptures than we do, it causes us to devote ourselves to greater study.

The following are some suggestions for applying

the Word of God to others.

Reconcile men to God. Our task is not to convince men of our doctrine, but to reconcile men to God. Paul taught that God has "given to us the ministry of reconciliation," that God has "committed unto us the word of reconciliation," and that "we are ambassadors for Christ" (II Corinthians 5:18-20). God wants us to bring men to Him. If we try to convert men to our beliefs, that is good. But if we try to introduce men to God, to get them on good terms with God, that is noble. And it is what God desires us to do.

We often want to add numbers to our churches, and that is worthy, but the more proper goal is to add men to His kingdom. Every attempt at soulwinning should be with the understanding that we are ambassadors for Jesus Christ. We represent Him.

Rest to the weary. Too often men attempt to win arguments when they should be offering a "cup of understanding." People who are weak and tired and frustrated with life seldom need impressive speeches from high-minded Christians. They need a warm hand, an embrace of genuine love and concern. "The LORD God hath given me the tongue of the learned, that I should know how to speak a word in season to him that is weary" (Isaiah 50:4).

Is it not significant that of all the terms Jesus could have used to refer to the Holy Spirit, such as power, magnificence, might, glory, or mystery, that he chose instead the word *Comforter*?

Perhaps the best verse of Scripture that points out the proper relationship we should have with others is found in Romans 14:1. Here is an example of people who could not agree on every subject. Issues were threatening to divide them. So Paul wrote, "Him that is weak in the faith receive ye, but not to doubtful disputations." He said later in the same discourse, "Hast thou faith? have it to thyself before

God" (Romans 14:22).

This takes us back to our priorities: first, apply the Word to ourselves; then apply it to others.

Paul taught that we should receive people who do not necessarily agree on every issue with us, and not to receive them just so we could argue the point and hope to convince them through our hospitality that we are right and they are wrong. But we should receive them because they are weak and need love, comfort, and rest. God has given us the ability to speak a word that will cause them to rest.

A Christian's duty toward others is not to strip them of every vestige of spiritual pride they may have, using his greater knowledge of the Scriptures. "And through thy knowledge shall the weak brother perish, for whom Christ died?" (I Corinthians 8:11). A Christian should use his knowledge to comfort others, to bring rest to them. When we have attempted to save the lost and to strengthen the weak, then we can say that we have properly applied the Word of God to others.

Test Your Knowledge

True or False

_____ 1. Hearing the Word of God is not applying or doing the Word of God.

_____ 2. The engrafted Word is the applied Word.

_____ 3. All doctrines claim to be based on the Word of God and are thus true.

_____ 4. The only reason one has for studying the Word of God is to prove doctrines.

_____ 5. Jesus overcame temptation by quoting verses of Scripture.

_____ 6. Doers of the Word soon discover new dimensions of life opening up to them.

_____ 7. The Bible's truths must first be applied to self before teaching them to others.

_____ 8. If you cannot spend thirty minutes a day reading the Bible, you might as well not read it at all.

_____ 9. Many people are so afraid of argument that they will not even talk about the Bible.

_____10. Talking about the Word of God sharpens our skill in using it.

Apply Your Knowledge

Create a small, simple chart with four headings across the top or down the left side: Prayer, Fasting, Bible Reading, and Witnessing. Keep an approximate record of how many minutes are spent each day in each area of Christian discipline. In the case of fasting, mark the chart by the day or half day.

The purpose of this exercise is not to become mechanical in our devotion to God, but rather to beat the devil at his feeble arguments. If we only have five minutes to pray, he says, "You don't have enough time to pray. You have only five minutes."

What we must realize is that five minutes of prayer is better than nothing! If it is given sincerely and whole-heartedly to God, He accepts it the same as an hour.

Keeping this chart for a few weeks will help you to evaluate and discipline your devotional life to God in a more effective way.

Expand Your Knowledge

If possible, locate a set of plans or blueprints for a house or building and observe them. Notice how every area of construction has been planned and coordinated. Keep the plans handy during your study of chapter thirteen.

Read also the Scriptures located under "Start With the Scriptures" for the next chapter.

Doctrine— God's Blueprint for Living 13

"Take heed unto thyself, and unto the doctrine; continue in them: for in doing this thou shalt both save thyself, and them that hear thee."
I Timothy 4:16

Start with the Scriptures

Mark 7:7
Acts 2:42
Romans 6:17; 16:17
II John 1-13
II Timothy 3:10; 4:3-6
Titus 1:9
Hebrews 6:1-2

The Bible is a wonderful gift from God. Through this study we have discovered its origin from the mind of God through the hands of men. We have witnessed its complexity, and yet admired its simplicity. We have learned ways to study it, and ways to apply it to our daily lives.

We should also understand its purpose. It is God's gift of instructions—doctrines—by which He intends man to live. It is God's blueprint for living!

Doctrine is a subject that is largely misunderstood.

It has sometimes received a bad name among men who have not accepted it for what it simply is.

Doctrine Defined

The word *doctrine* comes from Greek and Hebrew words which mean "instruction, or that which is taught." To some people, the mention of the word doctrine summons images of dour, long-faced, dark-robed administrators of the law. It should not. If doctrine is defined as "that which one teaches," then literally everyone has a doctrine. Parents give their doctrine to their children every time they correct their manners. School teachers give their doctrine every time they instruct a child in proper mathematics. Policemen enforce their doctrine in every ticket they write. Judges administer their doctrine each time they preside over court. Preachers dispense their doctrine in every sermon they preach. And the Bible offers its doctrines to anyone who will venture into its pages.

Denominational Doctrines

Do religious movements have doctrines? Of course they do. By the definition of doctrine, we have already shown that everyone has a doctrine. Religious groups all claim to teach the doctrines of the Bible, and in some measure they all do. However, each religious body interprets certain verses of Scripture different from what others do, and they teach their own interpretation. Each claims to teach only what the Bible teaches, yet each teaches different doctrines, based on their interpretation of the Scriptures.

Aside from organized church bodies, many independent churches exist. Some of them are easily identified with a major religious body, but many of them deliberately advertise that they are not associated with a particular organization. Advertising for such a church might read, "Interdenominational; All Faiths Worship Here."

At first glance, an interdenominational church may seem like an ideal situation to some people because they do not understand the nature of varied religious groups or the purpose of doctrine. In reality, it is impossible for people of all beliefs to worship together unless they are willing to lose some of their beliefs and, in so doing, take on the identity of the "interdenominational" church they attend.

To attend the church that claims to be nondenominational is to accept its doctrine, and the doctrine of many such churches is that one's personal beliefs are not critical to his salvation. For example, a church may teach that one member can believe baptism is essential for salvation and another member can believe baptism is only a voluntary act of worship; the real doctrine that is practiced is that both can be saved because it really does not matter what they believe.

But it does matter what a person believes! The Bible was given to us so that we might know how to live, and it must be obeyed in order to obtain salvation. If one's beliefs are unimportant to God, there is really no need for the Bible to exist. God gave the Bible because He had a plan for man to follow, and His plan is found within the pages of His Book.

Every honest church body (and independent church) has its interpretation of the Bible, and teaches the same. Can they all be so different and all of them still be right? The answer is obvious. Peter wrote that no prophecy of Scripture was of any private interpretation (II Peter 1:20). He went on to relate, "There shall be false teachers among you, who privily shall bring in damnable heresies, even denying the Lord that bought them, and bring upon themselves swift destruction. And many shall follow their pernicious ways; by reason of whom the way of truth shall be evil spoken of. And through covetousness shall they with feigned words make merchandise of you" (II Peter 2:1-3).

In light of these verses, no honest Christian can trust his denominational background to save him. Nor can he assume that because his religious organization is old and established it must be right. There is only one doctrine that is right, and it belongs to no exclusive organization. It is the doctrine of the Bible!

Every man must "work out [his] own salvation with fear and trembling" (Philippians 2:12). That does not excuse him from the necessity of attending church. It means that he must be certain that he is attending a church that teaches the doctrines of the Bible. He is responsible to know. He should study the Bible and verify every doctrine of his church with the Word of God.

Devoted to Doctrine

From the definition we have studied, it should be obvious that the Bible is doctrine from Genesis through Revelation. "All scripture is given by inspiration of God, and is profitable for doctrine..." (II Timothy 3:16). When doctrine is correctly defined and understood, every true Christian embraces it. If he loves God, he must also love God's Word. If he loves God's Word, he must also love doctrine.

The Apostle Paul was devoted to doctrine. He wrote to Timothy and instructed him to preach the doctrine (II Timothy 4:2). He wrote to the church at Rome and commended them for obeying the doctrine (Romans 6:17). Giving Titus instructions for elders and bishops, he said they should obey and teach doctrine (Titus 1:9). He told the perplexing Corinthians that he could profit them with doctrine (I Corinthians 14:6). Paul understood the meaning and value of doctrine, and he was devoted to it.

John was devoted to Jesus Christ. Love, faith, and truth are recurring themes in his writings. John knew that to love God was to love His doctrine; he wrote, "For this is the love of God, that we keep his commandments [doctrines]: and his commandments are not grievous" (I John 5:3).

When a person understands that all Scripture is given to us by God, and that all Scripture is God's blueprint for his life, he cannot help but be devoted to doctrine.

Developing Doctrine

It is imperative that Christians master the truths in the Bible. Those who have studied it for years and have heard countless sermons preached from it may feel comfortable between its covers. But a newcomer to the Bible is often intimidated by the copious books and chapters, and finds himself bewildered before he begins to study it. He does not know where to start.

A look back through the chapters of this book will help the student of the Bible know how to be selective in his study of the Bible. The methods of study suggested herein should also be very helpful to a new reader of the Word of God.

As an additional aid to discovering true Bible doctrines, consider the manner in which a builder erects a new building. We will follow his progress step-by-step and apply his techniques of building beautiful buildings to our challenge of building beautiful lives through following God's blueprint.

The builder receives the blueprints from the architect who designed the building. Nothing can be done until the drawings are complete, and the builder has them in his hand.

The world has received the completed set of plans from the Master Architect. The Bible contains every instruction necessary for making a life exactly what God wants it to be.

He looks over the entire set of plans to familiarize himself with the type of building the architect has in mind. He looks at plot plans, foundation plans, framing plans, plumbing plans, electrical plans, roofing plans, elevation drawings, and the colorful rendering of what the finished building is supposed to look like. He is a long way from the finished product, but he holds in his hands a picture of how it should look.

A glance over the whole Bible will give an individual a glimpse of what God intends for him to be. From Moses' law and the Old Testament characters, to the life of Christ and the Apostles' doctrine, that person begins to see the character God wants him to be. He may still be a long way from the finished product, but at least he knows what God is expecting of him.

Now the builder must determine the stages in which the building will be erected. First things first! The location must be precise before the first shovel can hit the ground, so from the plot plan the surveyors will determine the location of every corner.

We must be in the right location. Are we in a church that teaches the truth? If so, we should stay right where we are. Christians ought to beware of changing churches for petty reasons. They should not be unstable. God has begun a work in them and has placed them where they need to be. If problems come, they simply take care of the problems and stay put. They should avoid opportunities that come along which will cause them to have to relocate their church membership. If they are growing Christians, they need to allow God to finish the product.

Once the location has been determined, the builder is ready to begin a foundation. Perhaps the most important part of the whole building is the foundation. The prettiest walls will be of little value if they crumble because they were built on a weak foundation. The shovels must dig deep trenches, the steel must be strong, and the pouring must be done right if the finished product will bring any glory to the builder.

We must lay foundational doctrines before we do anything else. What are the foundational doctrines? The writer of Hebrews names six of them in Hebrews 6:1-2. We should consider each of them briefly:

- *Repentance.* Literally this means turning around from one way of living and making up our minds that we are going to live God's way. Have we made up our mind to serve God at any cost? This foundation must be laid before we concern ourselves with the outside of the building. A Christian should make up his mind that he will make his life conform to the image of Christ through His Word.

- *Baptisms.* Have we been baptized in water (immersed) in the name of Jesus Christ? We must be to know salvation. Before anything else can be built, this basic foundation must be laid. If a person has not been baptized, he should make haste to be baptized in the name of Jesus Christ. It is also essential that he be baptized with the Holy Spirit. It is a foundational doctrine. It is prerequisite to the virtues of spiritual living. We should be filled with the Spirit!

- *Faith.* "Without faith it is impossible to please [God]: for he that cometh to God must believe that he is, and that he is a rewarder of them that diligently seek him" (Hebrews 11:6). This is foundational material! Faith in God must first be established. We should believe that He will do everything He said He would do.

- *Laying on of hands.* We should submit ourselves to the prayers of the elders. We can call for the ministry to pray over us, anointing us with oil, and laying hands on us (Mark 16:17-18; James 5:14).
- *Resurrection of the dead.* A Christian will live again. This life is not the only life; it is but a vapor that will vanish in a while (James 4:14). When this one is over, another one is going to begin. We will live again!
- *Eternal judgment.* Someone once said that every sin was born of unbelief and that if a man really believed he would give an account for every deed, he would not sin. Every man is going to give an account. There is a judgment coming. We should believe it. "For if we sin wilfully after that we have received the knowledge of the truth, there remaineth no more sacrifice for sins, But a certain fearful looking for of judgment" (Hebrews 10:26).

These foundational doctrines should be firmly established in our hearts and minds.

After the foundation is ready, the builder is ready to erect the walls and the roof. The skeleton goes up first; the coverings will come later.

There are many structural doctrines, critical to the completion of a beautiful life. Consider a few:
- *The oneness of the Godhead.* There are not three persons in the Godhead, but rather, "in him [Jesus] dwelleth all the fulness of the Godhead bodily" (Colossians 2:9).
- *Spiritual gifts.* God gifted His church with supernatural power called the gifts of the Spirit.
- *The Second Coming of Christ.* Jesus Christ is taking His church out of the world in the Rapture, but He is going to establish one more dispensation upon this earth—the Millennium.
- *Good works.* James wrote, "I will shew thee my faith by my works" (James 2:18), and "faith without works is dead" (James 2:20).

- *Holiness.* "Follow peace with all men, and holiness, without which no man shall see the Lord" (Hebrews 12:14). Holiness of heart and character is an essential structural doctrine.
- *Forgiveness.* "But if ye forgive not men their trespasses, neither will your Father forgive your trespasses" (Matthew 6:15).
- *Brotherly love.* "If a man say, I love God, and hateth his brother, he is a liar: for he that loveth not his brother whom he hath seen, how can he love God whom he hath not seen? And this commandment have we from him, That he who loveth God love his brother also" (I John 4:20-21).
- *Freedom from sin.* "For the law of the Spirit of life in Christ Jesus hath made me free from the law of sin and death" (Romans 8:2).

There are many other doctrines that are vital to God's work in the church. The best way to learn of them is by going to a Bible-believing church and hearing the preached Word of God. "It pleased God by the foolishness of preaching to save them that believe" (I Corinthians 1:21).

Finally, after the foundation, the walls, and the roof have all been completed, the builder is ready to put on the trim, the paint, and the finishing decor. The actual glory of the building may lie in its solid foundation, but the visible glory that will be seen by men is applied in the last stages of the building.

Prayer, faith, and devotion to the doctrines of the Word of God may not always be visible traits of a Christian, but after establishing the right foundational doctrines, these finishing touches should also be added. Then everyone will readily recognize who the real Builder of that person's life is.

Doctrine That Decorates

A novice builder is often so anxious to get to the

finished product that he cuts corners in order to hurry his project. He will regret it if he does, however, for his building will not last.

Sometimes novice Christians are so anxious to see the finished product that they also try to cut corners.

Prayer might not seem as important to them as their appearance. They may spend more time dressing the body to appear holy than they spend preparing the spirit to receive the gifts of God.

Is the outward appearance important to God? Does He care how we dress, what we eat, how we entertain ourselves?

Just as a builder cares about the final appearance of his building, God cares about the appearance of His people. Our clothing styles, our hair, our habits, everything about us is important to Him.

Nothing is more beautiful to God than a modest, well-behaved, well-groomed person whose heart is rich in faith and love toward God. God sees the heart, however, and if He sees a person who has a holy appearance but whose heart is unholy, it is like seeing a beautiful house that is only a facade—a stage front built only for a drama set. It cannot be lived in, but it certainly is pretty to look at.

God wants to see a person who is in the process of developing proper priorities in doctrine, someone who is following His blueprint carefully. First, that person is learning to apply the foundational doctrines. He is developing a prayer life; he is discovering real faith; he is gaining knowledge by going to church and hearing preaching.

As he progresses, visible signs will begin to show. His clothing will begin to reflect a pure heart. His hair will begin to reflect a submissive spirit. His choices of friends will begin to reflect his friendship with the true Friend. The kind of entertainment he seeks will begin to reflect a clean heart.

But all of these visible signs are the decoration

that comes after the foundation, the walls, and the roof have all been built. They will be the crowning glory of the building God began in the heart.

Test Your Knowledge

1. _____ is a subject that is largely misunderstood.
2. *Doctrine* means "_____" or "that which is taught."
3. If one's beliefs are unimportant to _____, there is really no need for the _____ even to have been given to us.
4. No honest Christian can trust his _____ background to save him.
5. A Christian should study the Bible and _____ every _____ of his church with the Word of God.
6. The Apostle _____ was devoted to doctrine.
7. It is imperative that _____ master the truths in the Bible.
8. The world has received the Bible, the completed set of plans from the Master _____.
9. When a builder is ready to begin construction, he begins with the _____.
10. God cares about the _____ of His people.

Apply Your Knowledge

The Bible is our "blueprint" for living. Spend a few minutes thinking about the following activities and number them in order of what you feel are your present priorities. Try to be honest with yourself.

_____ House chores
_____ Spending time with family members
_____ Personal recreation

_____ Family recreation
_____ Church services
_____ Church activities (socials, etc.)
_____ Prayer
_____ Fasting
_____ Bible reading
_____ Meditation
_____ Reading (other than the Bible)
_____ Occupation

Now looking back, do you feel you need to change any of your priorities? Are they scriptural? Are they practical? Could you benefit by placing more emphasis in some area?

It is good on occasion to evaluate ourselves and determine our spiritual progress. There is nothing wrong with giving ourselves a check-up.

Expand Your Knowledge

For further personal or group study, consider the other volumes of the Word Aflame Elective Series. A list of titles is on page 2.